CUMBRIA LIBRARIES
3800304675854 6

Scarecrow Studies in Young Adult Literature
Series Editor: Patty Campbell

Scarecrow Studies in Young Adult Literature is intended to continue the body of critical writing established in Twayne's Young Adult Authors Series and to expand it beyond single-author studies to explorations of genres, multicultural writing, and controversial issues in young adult (YA) reading. Many of the contributing authors of the series are among the leading scholars and critics of adolescent literature, and some are YA novelists themselves.

The series is shaped by its editor, Patty Campbell, who is a renowned authority in the field, with a thirty-year background as a critic, lecturer, librarian, and teacher of YA literature. Patty Campbell was the 2001 winner of the ALAN Award, given by the Assembly on Adolescent Literature of the National Council of Teachers of English for distinguished contribution to YA literature. In 1989 she was the winner of the American Library Association's Grolier Award for distinguished service to young adults and reading.

1. *What's So Scary about R. L. Stine?* by Patrick Jones, 1998.
2. *Ann Rinaldi: Historian and Storyteller*, by Jeanne M. McGlinn, 2000.
3. *Norma Fox Mazer: A Writer's World*, by Arthea J. S. Reed, 2000.
4. *Exploding the Myths: The Truth about Teens and Reading*, by Marc Aronson, 2001.
5. *The Agony and the Eggplant: Daniel Pinkwater's Heroic Struggles in the Name of YA Literature*, by Walter Hogan, 2001.
6. *Caroline Cooney: Faith and Fiction*, by Pamela Sissi Carroll, 2001.
7. *Declarations of Independence: Empowered Girls in Young Adult Literature, 1990–2001*, by Joanne Brown and Nancy St. Clair, 2002.
8. *Lost Masterworks of Young Adult Literature*, by Connie S. Zitlow, 2002.
9. *Beyond the Pale: New Essays for a New Era*, by Marc Aronson, 2003.
10. *Orson Scott Card: Writer of the Terrible Choice*, by Edith S. Tyson, 2003.
11. *Jacqueline Woodson: "The Real Thing,"* by Lois Thomas Stover, 2003.

12. *Virginia Euwer Wolff: Capturing the Music of Young Voices*, by Suzanne Elizabeth Reid, 2003.
13. *More Than a Game: Sports Literature for Young Adults*, Chris Crowe, 2004.
14. *Humor in Young Adult Literature: A Time to Laugh*, by Walter Hogan, 2005.
15. *Life Is Tough: Guys, Growing Up, and Young Adult Literature*, by Rachelle Lasky Bilz, 2004.
16. *Sarah Dessen: From Burritos to Box Office*, by Wendy J. Glenn, 2005.
17. *American Indian Themes in Young Adult Literature*, by Paulette F. Molin, 2005.
18. *The Heart Has Its Reasons: Young Adult Literature with Gay/Lesbian/Queer Content, 1969–2004*, by Michael Cart and Christine A. Jenkins, 2006.
19. *Karen Hesse*, by Rosemary Oliphant-Ingham, 2005.
20. *Graham Salisbury: Island Boy*, by David Macinnis Gill, 2005.
21. *The Distant Mirror: Reflections on Young Adult Historical Fiction*, by Joanne Brown and Nancy St. Clair, 2006.
22. *Sharon Creech: The Words We Choose to Say*, by Mary Ann Tighe, 2006.
23. *Angela Johnson: Poetic Prose*, by KaaVonia Hinton, 2006.
24. *David Almond: Memory and Magic*, by Don Latham, 2006.

David Almond

Memory and Magic

Don Latham

Scarecrow Studies in Young Adult Literature, No. 24

SCARECROW PRESS, INC.
Lanham, Maryland • Toronto • Oxford
2006

SCARECROW PRESS, INC.

Published in the United States of America
by Scarecrow Press, Inc.
A wholly owned subsidiary of
The Rowman & Littlefield Publishing Group, Inc.
4501 Forbes Boulevard, Suite 200, Lanham, Maryland 20706
www.scarecrowpress.com

PO Box 317
Oxford
OX2 9RU, UK

Copyright © 2006 by Don Latham

All rights reserved. No part of this publication may be reproduced, stored in a retrieval system, or transmitted in any form or by any means, electronic, mechanical, photocopying, recording, or otherwise, without the prior permission of the publisher.

British Library Cataloguing in Publication Information Available

Library of Congress Cataloging-in-Publication Data

Latham, Don, 1959–
David Almond : memory and magic / Don Latham.
p. cm. — (Scarecrow studies in young adult literature ; 24)
Includes bibliographical references and index.
ISBN-13: 978-0-8108-5500-7 (alk. paper)
ISBN-10: 0-8108-5500-3 (alk. paper)
1. Almond, David, 1951—Criticism and interpretation. 2. Young adult literature, English—History and criticism. I. Title. II. Series.

PR6051.L588Z75 2006
823'.914—dc22

2006002300

∞™ The paper used in this publication meets the minimum requirements of American National Standard for Information Sciences—Permanence of Paper for Printed Library Materials, ANSI/NISO Z39.48-1992.
Manufactured in the United States of America.

To Eliza Dresang,
an extraordinary mentor and friend

Contents

Chronology		ix
Chapter 1	Memory and Magic	1
Chapter 2	Beyond the Bounds: *Counting Stars*	15
Chapter 3	Extraordinary Beings: *Skellig*, Novel and Play	33
Chapter 4	The Game Called Death: *Kit's Wilderness*	51
Chapter 5	Damaged Children: *Heaven Eyes*	65
Chapter 6	The Forests of the Night: *Wild Girl, Wild Boy*; *Secret Heart*; and *Kate, the Cat and the Moon*	79
Chapter 7	At the Gates of Hell: *The Fire-Eaters*	97
Chapter 8	Gods and Monsters: *Clay*	115
Chapter 9	Afterword: Magical Realism Revisited	129
Bibliography		133
Index		143
About the Author		151

~

Chronology

1951 Born May 15 in Newcastle upon Tyne, England, to James Arthur and Catherine Barber Almond

1959 Younger sister Barbara dies

1966 Father dies on Boxing Day

1974–1982 First marriage

1975 Graduates from the University of East Anglia with a B.A. (honors)

1982 Relationship with Sara Jane Palmer begins

1984 *Mickey and the Emperor* (children's play) produced at Washington Arts Centre

1985 *Sleepless Nights* (short stories)

1987–1993 Editor of *Panurge* (fiction magazine)

1990 Mother dies

1997 *A Kind of Heaven* (short stories)

1998 Daughter, Freya Grace, born; *Skellig* (novel), United Kingdom

1999 *Kit's Wilderness* (novel), United Kingdom; *Skellig* (novel), United States

2000 *Heaven Eyes* (novel), United Kingdom; *Counting Stars* (short stories), United Kingdom; *Kit's Wilderness* (novel), United States

2001 *Wild Girl, Wild Boy* (play) opens February 10 at Lyric Theatre, Hammersmith, London (director, Michael Dalton); *Secret Heart* (novel), United Kingdom; *Heaven Eyes* (novel), United States

2002 *Wild Girl, Wild Boy* (play), published United Kingdom; *Where Your Wings Were* (short stories), United Kingdom; *Secret Heart* (novel), United States; *Counting Stars* (short stories), United States; *Secret Heart* (play) opens at the Royal Exchange Theatre, Manchester (adapted by Amanda Dalton; director, Wils Wilson)

2003 *The Fire-Eaters* (novel), United Kingdom; *Skellig* (play) opens November 21 at the Young Vic Theatre, London (director, Trevor Nunn); *Skellig* (play), published United Kingdom

2004 *Kate, the Cat and the Moon* (picture book), United Kingdom (illustrator, Stephen Lambert); *The Fire-Eaters* (novel), United States

2005 *Clay* (novel), United Kingdom; *Heaven Eyes* (play) opens at Edinburgh Fringe Festival in August

CHAPTER ONE

~

Memory and Magic

Much like the mysterious, angelic creature found living in a dilapidated garage in his first novel, David Almond appeared to come out of nowhere.[1] He burst upon the young adult literary scene in 1998 with his book *Skellig*, which won the Whitbread Children's Book of the Year Award in England and, upon its publication in the United States (1999), was named a Michael L. Printz Honor Book. He followed up that initial success with *Kit's Wilderness* (1999/2000), winning a Smarties Silver Award and the Michael L. Printz Award. Subsequent books have garnered equal accolades: *Heaven Eyes* (2000/2001) was short-listed for the Whitbread Children's Book of the Year Award, while *The Fire-Eaters* (2003/2004) won both the Smarties Book Prize and the Whitbread Award. Almond's apparently sudden success, however, belies the years of hard work he spent writing short stories and editing a fiction magazine, years in which he honed his craft and developed the voice and sensibility that come through so powerfully in his young adult novels.

Born in 1951 in the former coal-mining town of Newcastle upon Tyne, Almond displayed even at an early age the telltale signs of someone who would most likely become a writer. As a baby, he gurgled happily as sheets of newspaper rolled off the presses in his uncle's printing shop. As a child, he loved to listen to his large Catholic family tell stories and sing songs, and he was enthralled by the gossip at the local coffee shop. Like many children, he says that he and his friends enjoyed scaring one another with ghost stories, and one can imagine a young David trying to outdo his mates by fabricating the most frightening story of all. A budding author even as a child, David wrote stories and sewed them together into little books.[2]

Almond has said that he did not care for school, especially after he turned eleven and entered secondary school. In fact, by the time he was thirteen, he had become quite disenchanted with school. When people nowadays talk to him about the so-called golden age of education, he tells them about his experiences with some "awful" teachers, like the sadistic Mr. Todd in *The Fire-Eaters*.[3] At the same time, he loved the local library as much as he hated school, and when he was not racing around on the soccer field, he could be found there buried in a book. This branch library, he has said, was his "field of dreams," a small unprepossessing place that nevertheless contained "a treasure trove" of materials to fire the imagination.[4] It was here that he discovered the writer who would become his "first mentor": Ernest Hemingway. Through reading Hemingway's short story "A Clean, Well-Lighted Place," Almond recognized not just that he wanted to be a writer, but that he wanted to be a particular kind of writer. As he describes it, "In a clean, well-lighted place I read 'A Clean, Well-Lighted Place,' and my life was changed forever."[5] He recalls spending many a day in the library, dreaming that one day he would see books on the shelves with his name on the spines.[6]

Almond did, of course, grow up to see books on library shelves with his name on the spines—and numerous award medallions on the covers—books filled with mystery and magic as well as darkness and death. This complex mixture of motifs can be traced to two formative influences in young David's life: the teachings of the Catholic Church and the untimely deaths of his father and younger sister. Almond recalls being frightened as a child by "the awful threats and glorious promises" in the stories told by the Irish priests in his local parish church.[7] No doubt he heard similar stories in the Catholic school he attended, which perhaps accounts for his strong distaste for school. These fire-and-brimstone stories, heard both at school and at church, account, in part, for the brooding darkness evident in his stories and novels. The darkness can also be attributed to the loss of his baby sister Barbara when David was seven years old, and the loss of his father to cancer (on Boxing Day, 1966) when David was fifteen.[8] Not surprisingly, then, death is a palpable presence in each of Almond's young adult novels. Other formative influences evident in the books include Almond's large and close-knit family; the people, customs, and dialects of Newcastle upon Tyne; and, of course, the town itself, a place that, according to Almond, "had everything necessary for the imagination."[9]

Growing up, David was particularly close to his grandfather, a large man of very few words. Always dressed in a dark suit, regardless of the weather, he often took David to the Newcastle open-air market, where they once saw an escapologist balancing a massive cart wheel on his forehead, sticking himself with needles, and breaking out of chains.[10] Many years later, this man would become the basis for the character of McNulty in *The Fire-Eaters*. David also spent a great deal of time at his grandfather's allotment (a portion of land set aside by civic authorities for cultivation[11]), where he helped tend the flowers and vegetables. As Almond himself has admitted, the time they spent together "shar[ing] long easy silences" might seem "pretty aimless," yet in many ways those experiences were preparing him to become a writer.[12] His grandfather and the allotment would make their way into the story "Chickens" in *Counting Stars*. The image of the allotment would be used as a metaphor for the creative imagination—a literal "field of dreams"—in the play *Wild Girl, Wild Boy*. And an adolescent boy's close relationship with his grandfather would become a major focus of the novel *Kit's Wilderness*. In that allotment, "between the houses of Fleming Gardens and Windy Ridge,"[13] seeds were being sown in young David's imagination that would one day flower in his literary works.

Upon leaving home, Almond enrolled at the University of East Anglia, in Norwich, some 200 miles south of his hometown.[14] He eventually took a B.A. degree, graduating with honors. In his last year at university, he got married, and this marriage would last eight years.[15] Upon graduation, he knew that he wanted to be a writer, but needed some way of supporting himself while writing. He worked a variety of odd jobs, including postman and brush salesman, before becoming a teacher.[16] During the course of his somewhat brief teaching career, he taught primary, adult, and special education students. Of the three, he found his work with special education students to be by far the most rewarding.[17] Nevertheless, in 1982 he resigned from his full-time job in order to devote himself to writing. At this time he also met and fell in love with Sarah Jane Palmer. Over the next sixteen years, Almond paid his literary dues, writing for an adult audience: he wrote stories that appeared in little magazines, published two collections of short stories (*Sleepless Nights* in 1985 and *A Kind of Heaven* in 1997), worked as the editor of the fiction magazine *Panurge*, finished one novel that he could not get published, worked on another that he never finished, and wrote a collection of stories set in his boyhood hometown of Newcastle.[18] Then in 1998, at about the time *Skellig* was published, David and Sarah Jane had a child, Freya Grace.[19] It is to Freya Grace that *Skellig* is dedicated.

In his third collection of stories, initially entitled *Stories from the Middle of the World*, Almond focused on his own childhood and adolescence, depicted in stories that he has described as "half-real, half-imaginary."[20] As it turned out, the process of writing these autobiographical stories paved the way for the creation of *Skellig*. Almond has stated in interviews that, once he had written the Newcastle stories, *Skellig* came unexpectedly and very easily.[21] The novel was widely praised by reviewers in both England and the United States, and, as already noted, it garnered numerous awards. In the process, Almond had acquired fame and success and had become a young adult writer. It was almost as if he had emerged from the long period of literary gestation fully formed as the young adult writer he was always meant to be. Perhaps this is the stuff of magic after all, but it certainly did not come without considerable talent and a great deal of hard work. In many ways, Almond had been preparing for this moment all of his life.

Early Works

In addition to serving as the editor of *Panurge*, Almond published a number of short stories in small fiction magazines. These stories, many of which were subsequently published in *Sleepless Nights* and *A Kind of Heaven*, were intended for an adult audience. The press runs were very small—about 500 each—and both volumes are not easy to find now.[22] Many of the stories reveal that Almond already had an interest in the themes and issues that would surface later in his young adult works. He has described several of the stories in *Sleepless Nights* as "playful" works that "obviously came from my reading of people like Márquez and Borges."[23] Moreover, several of the stories also deal with either childhood or adolescence. Overall, though, Almond now feels that many of the stories in *Sleepless Nights* lack control and are relentlessly dark.[24] The focus on adolescence is even more prevalent in *A Kind of Heaven*, although the viewpoint is typically that of an adult looking back. These stories contain ghosts and ghostly memories, evocations of family and place, a brooding sense of darkness and death, and a fascination with and sympathy for marginalized, and often grotesque, characters.

The opening, and title, story in *A Kind of Heaven* is set in 1962 and depicts a boy and his mother traveling to the market in Newcastle, where they see an escapologist performing. The names are different, but otherwise the characters foreshadow those in the opening scene of *The Fire-Eaters*. In "A Kind of Heaven," it is the mother rather than the father who is ill, and the escapologist is said to have served with the boy's father in Egypt rather than Burma. But the characters and the basic plot are the same. The final story, "1962," is also set during the Cuban Missile Crisis, and it too prefigures the characters and themes of *The Fire-Eaters*. In this story, a working-class boy named Askew torments a new boy named Daniel and also a tramp who has taken up residence in the nearby dunes.

"Lucy Blue" is an old-fashioned ghost story, as is "Spotlight." "Lucy Blue" tells the story of an outcast, a woman whose father first abandoned her and then returned only to kill her mother and abuse his daughter. When the narrator, a childhood friend of Lucy's, returns to help the now grown Lucy kill her father, she sees not only Lucy in the house, but also the ghost of Lucy's mother. "Spotlight" is the story of a game of hide-and-seek played at night using only a flashlight. The game is played on the wilderness, a landscape riddled with old mine pits and shafts, but a perfect place for such a game because the children can hide there by covering themselves with sod. When one child's overly concerned mother goes looking for him in the wilderness, she sees dozens of children pushing their way up out of the ground like corpses rising from their graves. The image foreshadows that of the ghost children in *Kit's Wilderness*, in which an abandoned mine pit also figures prominently.

"Where Your Wings Were" is included in *A Kind of Heaven* in almost exactly the same form as in *Counting Stars* (see chapter 2), and it reappears in the collection of stories *Where Your Wings Were*, which contains four of the stories from *Counting Stars* plus one additional story. Clearly, this is a story that Almond is fond of, combining as it does the memory of his dead younger sister, his mother's devout belief in angels, and his own emerging adolescent sexuality. The conceit of one's shoulder blades as being the place "where your wings were" reappears in *Skellig* as well, where it is used to show the presence of the extraordinary amid the ordinary realities of everyday life.

Almond has acknowledged that the stories in his two adult collections in many ways prefigure the characters and themes of his works for young adults in spite of the fact that, unlike his young adult novels, many of the "adult" stories have bleak and/or disturbing endings.[25] "Fiesta," for example, ends with a young boy, who has been neglected by his mother and her boyfriend, giving up in desperation and joining a group of fire-eaters. "Lucy Blue" ends with the narrator, Lucy's childhood friend, preparing to stab Lucy's derelict father. And "Dogs" ends with a boy imagining killing a dog and then dreaming of being transformed into a dog. Yet one can also see in many of these stories the lyrical, magical elements that make Almond's young adult works so moving and so appealing.

Major Themes

Almond's major concern is with the development of identity as an ongoing process that occurs in a series of borderlands—between childhood and adulthood, the natural and the supernatural, between life and death, and between past and present. A number of critics have labeled Almond's writing as being within the tradition known as magical realism. In interviews, Almond has both embraced this label and bristled against it.[26] Magical realism, as the name implies, is concerned with how the supernatural is manifested in everyday life. Even a cursory reading of his works will show that this is a theme Almond returns to again and again, exploring the presence of the mystical and the magical in ordinary places: the angel-like creature Skellig in a dilapidated garage; the precocious ghost boy Silky in an abandoned mine pit (*Kit's Wilderness*); the mysterious girl known as Heaven Eyes in the defunct printing works; and the blind soothsayer, Nanty Solo, in a run-down circus (*Secret Heart*). How the miraculous infuses everday life—and the special ability of young people to recognize that—is a major theme of Almond's books.

Related to that theme is a fascination with darkness and death. As Geraldine Brennan has pointed out, the game called Death, played by the main characters in *Kit's Wilderness*, can be seen as the symbolic center of Almond's opus.[27] Created by John Askew, an adolescent who dresses in black and wears a Megadeth tee shirt, the game involves children who descend into an abandoned mine pit each day to see who will be chosen to "die." The feigned deaths echo the actual deaths of children that occurred many years before when the mine was still in operation. By pretending to die, the children experience a deeper connection to their past while facing and gaining control over their fear of death. A preoccupation with death permeates Almond's books. In *Skellig*, Michael's baby sister has a serious, potentially fatal heart condition. In *Kit's Wilderness*, Kit's grandfather experiences the dissolution of his mind and faculties as his life slowly slips away. Older characters die in *Heaven Eyes* and *Secret Heart* as well, and *Counting Stars* contains the accounts of the deaths of Almond's father and baby sister. As is often the case in adolescent novels, encounters with death, while representing deep, emotional loss, also provide a way for the main characters to gain the maturity and insight needed to confront their own mortality and successfully negotiate the passage from childhood to adulthood.[28]

The importance of memory—of family, community, and place—is another prevalent theme in Almond's works. Kit, for example, in moving to Stoneygate, is returning to the place where his ancestors lived and worked. His growth as a young adult becomes closely intertwined with the discovery of his roots and his connection to the town and the wilderness of the title. The wilderness is the site of the abandoned coal mine and the place where the children play the game called Death.

Finally, a concern with the role of the creative imagination in the development of identity is evident in all of Almond's young adult works. His novels demonstrate his strong faith in the power of art in general and of stories in particular. Michael in *Skellig* and Kit in *Kit's Wilderness* are both writers of stories. John Askew is a gifted illustrator who collaborates with Kit while Allie Keenan is an exceptional actress. In Almond's books the development of selfhood involves an exploration of the inner world of the imagination, as is suggested by Joe's discovery of his tiger heart in *Secret Heart*. In his Michael L. Printz Award acceptance speech, Almond discussed the importance of imagination, self-reflection, and discovery: "Our children need to know . . . that living, achieving, and aspiring are . . . courageous imaginative acts. . . . We need to keep reminding ourselves and our children: slow down; wander through the wilderness inside yourself. . . . Take the time to dream, take the time to imagine."[29]

Magical Realism

In his use of magical realism, Almond is invoking a literary tradition that is both transnational and intertextual by nature. The term *magic realism* was first used by art critic Franz Roh in 1925 to characterize German post-Expressionist's return to a more realistic style of painting.[30] The term was then taken up by Alejo Carpentier in 1949, transformed into the phrase "Marvelous Real," and applied to a style of literature evident among a number of Latin American writers in the 1930s.[31] Since then the term has evolved into the term we know today as "magical realism," and as a style it is evident in the works of a variety of writers and other artists, not just in Latin America, but throughout the world. Neither strictly fantasy nor strictly realism, magical realism combines elements of both, revealing the presence of the extraordinary amid the ordinary realities of everyday life.

Although elements of the mode are evident throughout Almond's opus, his use of, and debt to, magical realism can be seen most clearly in his first young adult novel, *Skellig*, the story of an adolescent boy who finds a sick, tattered angel living in his family's dilapidated garage. This novel recalls a similar short story published in 1968 by Colombian writer Gabriel García Márquez, "A Very Old Man with Enormous Wings," subtitled "A Tale for Children." In this story a young couple, Pelayo and Elisenda, discover a bedraggled angel lying in their yard, the hapless victim of a torrential rainstorm. Almond has said that, although he had read García Márquez, he did not have the story consciously in mind when he began writing *Skellig*. However, about halfway into the novel, he suddenly realized the similarities between his book and García Márquez's short story—and realized that "A Very Old Man with Enormous Wings" was a "major influence" on his novel.[32] In terms of plot and imagery, the two works do display obvious parallels, but, at the same time, they employ magical realism toward very different ends.

García Márquez's focus is on adult characters, and children do not play a major role in the story. Almond's focus is on his adolescent characters, Michael and his friend Mina. But perhaps the most important difference between the two works lies in the fate of each angel. García Márquez's very old man is turned into a public spectacle, gawked at, mistreated, and kept on display like a caged animal. In contrast, Almond's angel remains known only to Michael and Mina. The text implies that Michael and Mina understand intuitively that revealing his existence to adults would likely bring upon Skellig the same sort of abuse and exploitation that García Márquez's old man suffers. Instead, they secretly care for him and nourish him back to health, and, as a result, come to recognize the extraordinary qualities within themselves.

In examining Almond's use of magical realism and its relationship to the themes of death, memory, creativity, and identity, it will be helpful to keep in mind Wendy B. Faris's five characteristics of magical realism:

1. An irreducible element of magic
2. A grounding in the phenomenal world, i.e., the realistic world
3. The reader's experience of unsettling doubts because of this mixture of the real and the fantastic
4. The near merging of two realms or worlds
5. Disruptions of traditional ideas about time, space, and identity[33]

These characteristics are evident in each of Almond's novels, to varying degrees. His skillful combination of an irreducible element of magic with a grounding in the real world can be seen in the character of Skellig himself: He has wings, is able to rise from the ground, and can perform miraculous healings. Yet, at the same time, he suffers from arthritis, he craves Chinese food, and he drinks bottles of beer. Michael initially experiences unsettling doubts about Skellig's existence, as does the reader. And we are never certain about Skellig's identity; even he seems uncertain about what exactly he is. *Kit's Wilderness* and *Heaven Eyes* merge two realms in showing how the world of the dead impinges on the world of the living. *Secret Heart* disrupts traditional notions about identity by depicting a boy who is able to transform himself into various beasts. And, while *The Fire-Eaters* is less magical than the other novels, it does, through its use of photographs, raise questions about identity, representation, and the impact of the past on the present. In many ways, *Counting Stars* and *Clay* are less magical as well, but they do contain kernels of many of the magical realist elements that Almond brings to fruition in subsequent works.

When asked what the use of magical realism allows him to accomplish as a writer, Almond has said that it gives him the opportunity to write "apparently very simply and very plainly" about "strange occurrences in a very direct and very realistic manner."[34] He has also said that magical realism allows him "to stay inside the real world" and yet still be able "to show the multifaceted nature of reality."[35] It might be argued that magical realism allows him to accomplish several other goals as well, related to specific thematic concerns. As Maggie Ann Bowers has noted, magical realist fiction is often set in rural areas and often involves the perspective of marginalized or "politically or culturally disempowered" people.[36] Almond himself has acknowledged that "the places and people that inhabit my stories have historically been pretty much excluded from mainstream English culture. To many cultured southerners, the northeast [of England] has been seen as a pretty barbaric place."[37] In employing magical realism to write about a marginalized place and people, Almond is joining a long tradition that includes Latin American, Indian, and African American writers, just to name a few. Furthermore, it could be argued that Almond's focus on adolescent characters is a concern with yet another kind of marginalization.

Indeed, two other aspects of magical realism seem apropos to Almond's concern with adolescence. One is the subversive and transgressive nature of magical realism as a literary mode.[38] The fact that both realism and magic are presented with the same seriousness within the text means that each is presented as equally valid. As a result, each mode tends to subvert the other.[39] At the same time, magical realism is transgressive in the sense that it is neither realism nor fantasy, but a third mode that encourages a multiplicity of interpretations.[40] Magical realism, by extension then, can serve to question "the assumptions of the dominant culture and particularly the notion of scientifically and logically determined truth."[41] In terms of Almond's work for adolescents, magical realism is a means for questioning the tenets of adult authority. Another connection between magical realism and adolescence can be found in Lois Parkinson Zamora and Wendy B. Faris's idea that magical realist texts "often situate themselves on liminal territory . . . in phenomenal and spiritual regions where transformation, metamorphosis, dissolution are common."[42] The term "liminal" is the adjectival form of the word "limen," which is defined literally as "the threshold of a physiological or psychological response."[43] But, as Zamora and Faris use the term in relation to magical realism, it refers more broadly to a transitional state between two other, more stable, states—between childhood and adulthood, for example, or between waking and sleeping, even between life and death. As such, the term "liminal" might be aptly applied to the "in-between" state of adolescence. And, in fact, one of Almond's key concerns is with the liminal territory of adolescent identity and the relationship between identity formation and the creative imagination.

Finally, magical realism may be seen as a natural progression from the kinds of magical stories most children read (or have read to them). Typically, these stories involve magic occurring for a finite period of time within a realistic setting. Children can thus "explore disruptions in their ordinary world secure in the knowledge that such magic and extraordinariness can be contained."[44] Magical realism's appeal for adult readers may stem from the fact that some adults "are simply reluctant to give up their childhood approach to stories."[45] In Almond's novels, there is clearly a celebration of this "childhood approach to stories" and the suggestion that adolescents need not give up that unique ability to see the magic, not just in texts, but in the world around them. Many of Almond's adult authority figures cannot see this magic, but most of his young characters can. He has said, "The world of children on the one hand is very plain and very ordinary but is also very magical and filled with a kind of sense of possibility."[46] In discussing *Skellig* with schoolchildren, he has discovered that "kids understand that something can be imaginary and real at the same time," whereas adults often insist on classifying Skellig, the character, as imaginary.[47]

A desire to preserve this kind of dual understanding in young people, coupled with a valorization of the creative imagination, is evident throughout Almond's works. Though the magic would not come into full blossom until *Skellig*, the seeds of magical realism were sown in his transitional work—his own liminal territory, if you will—*Counting Stars*.

Notes

1. Kathleen Odean described Almond's debut as "almost as magical as the novels he writes." See Kathleen Odean, "Mystic Man," *School Library Journal* 47.4 (2001): 48–52, *WilsonSelectPlus*, online, 1 June 2003.
2. "David Almond," *Contemporary Authors online*, Gale, 2003, *Literature Resource Center*, online, 23 January 2004.
3. David Almond, personal interview, 21 April 2005.
4. David Almond, "Fiction and Poetry Award Winner," *The Horn Book* 81.1 (2005): 33.
5. Almond, "Fiction and Poetry Award Winner," 34.
6. David Almond, "The 2001 Michael L. Printz Award Acceptance Speech," *Journal of Youth Services in Libraries* 14.4 (2001): 14–15, 23, *WilsonSelectPlus*, online, 13 February 2003.
7. "David Almond," *Contemporary Authors Online*.
8. Mark Mordue, "The Gentle Dreamer," *Sunday Age* (Melbourne), 1 June 2003: Agenda, 10, *Lexis-Nexis*, online, 3 June 2003; David Almond, personal e-mail, 13 May 2005.
9. "David Almond," *Contemporary Authors Online*.
10. Almond, "Fiction and Poetry Award Winner," 35.
11. "Allotment," def. 4, *The Oxford English Dictionary*, 2nd ed., (New York: Oxford University Press, 1989).
12. David Almond, "Afterword," *Wild Girl, Wild Boy: A Play* (London: Hodder Children's Books, 2002) 84–85.
13. Almond, "Afterword," 83.
14. Almond, personal interview.
15. Almond, personal e-mail.
16. David Almond, "A Note from the Author," *Skellig* (New York: Delacorte P, 1999) 183.
17. Almond, personal interview.
18. Almond, personal interview.
19. "David Almond," *Contemporary Authors Online*.
20. "David Almond," *Contemporary Authors Online*.
21. Elizabeth Devereaux, "Flying Starts," *Publishers Weekly* 26 (28 June 1999): 25, *Literature Resource Center*, online, 29 May 2003.
22. Almond, personal interview.
23. Almond, personal interview.

24. Almond, personal interview.
25. Almond, personal interview.
26. See, for example: Ilene Cooper, "The *Booklist* Interview," *Booklist* 96 (online, 2000): 898, *Literature Resource Center*, 4 June 2003, and Mordue, "The Gentle Dreamer."
27. Geraldine Brennan, "The Game Called Death: Frightening Fictions by David Almond, Philip Gross, and Lesley Howarth," *Frightening Fiction: R. L. Stine, Robert Westall, David Almond, and Others*, ed. Kimberley Reynolds, Geraldine Brennan, and Kevin McCarron (New York: Continuum, 2001) 93.
28. Roberta Seelinger Trites, *Disturbing the Universe: Power and Repression in Adolescent Literature* (Iowa City, IA: University of Iowa Press, 2000) 117, 119.
29. Almond, "The 2001 Michael L. Printz Award Acceptance Speech."
30. Franz Roh, "Magic Realism: Post-Expressionism," in Lois Parkinson Zamora and Wendy B. Faris's *Magical Realism: Theory, History, Community* (Durham, NC: Duke University Press, 1995) 15–31.
31. Alejo Carpentier, "On the Marvelous Real in America," in Zamora and Faris's *Magical Realism: Theory, History, Community*, 75–88.
32. Almond, personal interview.
33. Wendy B. Faris, *Ordinary Enchantments: Magical Realism and the Remystification of Narrative* (Nashville, TN: Vanderbilt University Press, 2004) 7.
34. Almond, personal interview.
35. Cooper, "The *Booklist* Interview."
36. Maggie Ann Bowers, *Magic(al) Realism* (New York: Routledge, 2004) 32–33.
37. Almond, "Fiction and Poetry Award Winner," 31–32.
38. Bowers, *Magic(al) Realism*, 67.
39. Bowers, *Magic(al) Realism*, 67.
40. Bowers, *Magic(al) Realism*, 67.
41. Bowers, *Magic(al) Realism*, 69.
42. Zamora and Faris, *Magical Realism*, 6.
43. "Limen," *The American Heritage Dictionary of the English Language*, 4th ed. (Boston: Houghton Mifflin, 2000).
44. Bowers, *Magic(al) Realism*, 104.
45. Bowers, *Magic(al) Realism*, 109.
46. Almond, personal interview.
47. Almond, personal interview.

CHAPTER TWO

~

Beyond the Bounds: *Counting Stars*

The Newcastle stories, although written before *Skellig*, were not published until after the success of *Skellig*, *Kit's Wilderness*, and *Heaven Eyes*, and, when the collection finally came out in 2000 (2002 in the United States), the title had been changed to *Counting Stars* and the book was marketed not to adults, as originally intended, but to adolescents. And two years after that, a subset of four stories from *Counting Stars* plus one additional story was published in the United Kingdom as *Where Your Wings Were*.[1] So, in terms of publication, *Counting Stars* is not the first work in Almond's young adult opus, but it is the first in terms of composition. For that reason, it will be useful to discuss it here because it serves as a transitional work between the adult books and the young adult books, and as such provides an introduction to many of the themes and images that permeate the adolescent novels. Like the novels, these stories focus on a strong sense of place, close family ties, the effects of loss through death, the importance of memory and stories for the developing adolescent, and a fascination with the presence of the mystical amid the ordinary aspects of everyday life. The overarching theme of the book is captured in one of the story titles: "Beating the Bounds." In many ways, the major focus of all of the stories is young David's experience of moving beyond the bounds, or testing the limits, of family, place, religion, and youth itself. At the same time, these stories represent the adult writer's experience of moving beyond the bounds of writing strictly for an adult audience and in the short story format. As Almond has said, after completing these stories, *Skellig* "just happened to me; it really did just come out of the blue as if it had been waiting."[2]

Because *Counting Stars* was published after Almond's first three young adult novels, reviewers had the luxury of hindsight by which to judge this collection. They noted the connections to his previously published works, but also commented on the adult viewpoint, the mature subject matter, and the fragmented chronology. Erica Wagner, writing in *The Times*, described the book as "a moving, perceptive collection that drifts back and forth over the shadowy border between fiction and autobiography, conjuring with brilliant clarity the elusive joys, sorrows and shames of childhood."[3] Noting that the stories were originally intended for adults—and that some were published in adult literary magazines—Wagner opined that younger readers might find them "somewhat disappointing," although older readers were sure to be enchanted. Hazel Rochman praised Almond for the "lyrical simplicity" with which he described "the miraculous in everyday life."[4] The reviewer for *Kirkus* found the stories "magical," but acknowledged that they were "not light or easy reading."[5] Elizabeth Bush, writing in *The Bulletin of the Center for Children's Books*, noted that, as with Almond's previous novels, "[s]omber mood and ethereal atmosphere again overshadow plot." She also commented on the "embittered" adult point of view found in the stories, although she felt that "older readers prepared to ponder darker dreams" would be well rewarded.[6] Gregory Maguire, who found the stories to be both "elliptical and epiphanic," felt that the collection would appeal more to people who were already fans of Almond's "gritty fabulism."[7] Interestingly, Philip Pullman, the highly regarded fantasy writer, felt that Almond was even better in this collection of stories than in his novels because the stories evinced a "firmly-rooted realism."[8] William McLoughlin, however, worried that the time and place of "this memory quilt" might be too far removed from the experiences of today's children.[9] In contrast, Sherrie Williams, reviewing the book for VOYA, found that the "nonlinear [narrative] patchwork . . . simply adds to the magical tone that is characteristic of [Almond's] work." She also described the language as "beautiful and poetic" and declared the book to be "memorable."[10]

The main characters in the stories are Almond's family, so it is fitting that the book is dedicated to all of them. Much like the stories in

James Joyce's *Dubliners* or Sherwood Anderson's *Winesburg, Ohio*, the stories are interwoven with common themes and images so that the collection functions as a consistent artistic whole, in many ways like a novel. As Almond makes clear in the introduction, these stories are unabashedly autobiographical, but they are not simply transcriptions of events from his childhood and adolescence; instead, "[l]ike all stories, they merge memory and dream, the real and the imagined, truth and lies" (xi). Almond's description of the workings of the literary imagination foreshadows themes that will resurface in his novels, in particular the roles of memory and magic and of truth and dreams in shaping the identity of the developing adolescent. He also makes explicit the important role stories play in helping to construct meaning out of the vagaries of life: these stories, he writes, "are an attempt to reassemble what is fragmented, to rediscover what has been lost" (xi). Writing thus proves to be "a kind of magic" (209).

In many ways, the eighteen stories in *Counting Stars* are an attempt to come to terms with three key losses Almond experienced growing up—the loss through death of his father and his infant sister, Barbara, and his loss of faith in the teachings of the Catholic Church. Recurring images and themes include angels and outcasts, the oppressiveness of the Church, journeys both inward and outward, the tension between the physical and the spiritual, and a strong sense of family and place. The trajectory of the stories takes us from "The Middle of the World," i.e., the kitchen of the Almond household, to "Beating the Bounds" at the boundaries of the community; from young David's exotic journey to "Jonadab" to his even more exotic—and erotic—adolescent vision of angels in "Where Your Wings Were." From a critical perspective, it is useful to consider the stories in thematic groups rather than consecutively, for then we can see the polyphonic nature of the collection, with multiple perspectives complementing one another.[11] The result is a more complex and nuanced view than any one of the stories conveys by itself.

Family and Place

The opening story, "The Middle of the World," introduces the family as a central, powerful force in the book and in young David's life. This story also exemplifies the classic structure of journey and return, and, as such, introduces a structural device that will appear throughout the book. The story begins at home with the Almond children gathered in their kitchen, and the youngest sister, Margaret, trying to identify the middle of the world. A typically inquisitive child, she then wonders, "'What's the middle of me?'" (1). Although she receives various answers from her family—her heart, her soul, her navel—she decides there really is no end to the world or middle. The story continues with the children (all except for Colin, the oldest, who must go to work) going to the cemetery to visit the graves of their sister Barbara, who died in 1959, and their father, James, who died in 1966. This is a journey, we are told, that the children do not often take, for they consider the dead to be in Heaven, not on earth. Once at the gravesite, the children read the inscription on the headstone, which introduces the angelic imagery that will be echoed in later stories in this collection and, most notably, in the novel *Skellig*: "Neither can they die any more, for they are equal unto the angels" (7). While the inscription points to the spiritual realm, David's thoughts turn paradoxically toward the physical, as he thinks of the decaying bodies and coffins and imagines family members who will be buried in this plot in years to come. The continuing, palpable presence of the dead father and sister in the lives of the other family members, along with the physicality of life, the connection to the past, and the cyclical nature of human existence are themes that recur in *Counting Stars* and in the novels as well.

Another motif is introduced here that appears in later stories, that of the eccentric outcast who appears to have a special connection to the mystical world. On the way to the cemetery and on the way back, the children encounter Daft Peter, a benign menace who makes fantastic claims. He says, for instance, that he can turn a fish into a bird, that he can teach the girls to fly, and that he can show the children the entrance to Hell through the cracks in the pavement in Felling Square. This character type, someone most people would label as "crazy," surfaces again in *Counting Stars*, in Miss Golightly ("The Baby"), Loosa Fine ("Loosa Fine"), and Jack Law ("Jack Law").

When the children return home, having visited the dead and encountered the somewhat comic guardian of the underworld, they once again gather at the kitchen table where they eat the warm bread with raisins. It is at this point that David realizes they are all "squeezed in tight in the middle of the world" (12). The kitchen, the traditional nexus of hearth and kin, *is* the center of the universe for this close-knit family as it is for many people, a place where love, conversation, joys, and sorrows are shared.

In the later story entitled "The Kitchen," Almond returns to these same themes, except that this gathering is strictly imaginative. The family, now apparently all grown and all still alive, gather in the kitchen to eat toast and talk about their lives. The father asks Margaret if she remembers when, as a very young girl, she asked him what the smallest place in the world was. The grown Margaret does not remember this incident, and the father does not remember how he responded to her typically childish question. However, he speculates that maybe the kitchen, with everyone present and everyone safe, is actually the smallest place in the world, echoing Almond's speculation in the opening story that the kitchen is the center of all existence. Barbara says that for her the grave turned out to be the smallest place. She goes on to say that she was afraid her memory would get lost. The others assure her that this did not happen. Her memory, according to the father, was comprised of "'[t]ruth and memories and dreams and bits made up'" (171), much like the stories in this collection.

As the family talk about death and memory, they hear children outside singing a song that recounts the months of the year, emphasizing the continual passage of time. The kitchen, the smallest place in the world, provides a welcome if temporary refuge from the ravages of time, a place where the family can tell stories that will bind them together. The power of stories and the power of the imagination make the "magical" kitchen of this second story just as real as—perhaps in some ways more real than—the kitchen of the more "realistic" first story. Whereas the first story focuses on the physicality of life and death, the second story focuses on the spiritual dimension, going so far as to suggest, in the father's words, that the kitchen constitutes a "'kind of Heaven'" (175). Clearly, it is liminal territory, both real and magical, where the family is sustained by the memories and stories that they share.

While these two stories deal with place in the sense of familial space, the second and third stories of the collection, "Counting the Stars" and "Beating the Bounds," deal with the issue of place in cosmic and geographic terms respectively. "Counting the Stars" unfolds as a diptych, with the first part telling the story of David's defiant refusal to observe Father O'Mahoney's edict against counting more than 100 stars. To count more, according to the priest, is to commit blasphemy by pretending to be capable of achieving knowledge that only God can possibly have. Counting beyond 100 places one in danger of committing a mortal sin. While David observed this prohibition for a time, as he grew older, he began to see it as an attempt on the priest's part to stifle the potentially "liberating effects" of education in order to insure the hold of the Church over its communicants (15). Accordingly, David begins to count far beyond 100, expressing his defiance over the priest and what he senses is a "worn-out religion" (15). He goes further, though, than simply exerting his own freedom and individuality when he forces his younger sister Catherine to watch and listen as he counts the stars beyond 100. The tears in her eyes suggest a myriad of emotions, including fear for her brother's soul and hurt because of his deliberate cruelty, but also sorrow in realizing that the priest was wrong and perhaps purposefully deceitful. David himself no longer feels proud or defiant, but merely ashamed and guilty for what he has done to his sister's tender beliefs. Before going to sleep he asks for forgiveness, not of his sister but of the silence into which he speaks.

The second part of the story describes in vivid detail the father's illness and eventual death. The family's prayers and the priest's visitations are to no avail as the father gradually weakens and his pain increases. In *Skellig* there are no priests, only ineffectual doctors who seem incapable of healing Michael's baby sister. In "Counting the Stars," doctors play a minor role; the priest is the more predominant representative of society's institutions, but his spiritual methods seem as ineffective as the rational, scientific methods of the doctors in *Skellig*. After the father's death, the priest's advice to David is to "'pray very hard'" (22). The story ends with David, Catherine, and Colin standing in the bitter cold outside the house, watching a meteor shower in which the falling stars are too numerous to count.

The juxtaposition of these two parts of the story, with the connecting threads of the priest and the stars, suggests at least two philosophical alternatives, both of which, I believe, are at work in the adolescent David's mind. One is that David has brought about his father's illness through his own arrogance and defiance of God and the Church. Although David as narrator never suggests this possibility, the implication is clearly there, at least in a subconscious way. One piece of evidence is the placement of two key statements. The first serves as the final statement in the section on counting the stars, and it describes David's guilt over forcing his defiance and skepticism on his sister. In the very next statement, the opening statement of the second section, Almond writes, "Soon afterward, our father became ill" (17). Although he never suggests that he was the cause of his father's illness, the juxtaposition of the two statements clearly raises the possibility that he thinks as much. David describes praying fervently throughout his father's illness, an action which indicates that, in spite of his earlier defiance of the priest's command, he has not totally abandoned the teachings of the Church although ultimately the prayers seem as ineffectual as the priest who encourages them. Another philosophical option, however, is that life and death are random, that there is no omnipotent force in the universe, that the world is hurling through a "wilderness" (23). In many ways this alternative is more frightening than the belief that there is a God who is punishing David for his intellectual pride. Ultimately, God or no God, David is unable to control life and death through either rationalism or religion. At the end of the story, David's place in the universe is one in which he is literally overwhelmed by the stars falling through the sky.

The companion story, "Beating the Bounds," deals not with the universal and metaphysical but rather with the local and the physical, i.e., the geographic boundaries of the town of Felling. The title refers to the practice, apparently Anglican rather than Roman Catholic, of marking out the boundaries of the town by beating the earth and then by beating the children so that they would remember where the boundaries were. The ceremony is reenacted every Ascension Day, the day when Christ ascended into Heaven, and its purpose, somewhat ironically, is to remind the participants of their own "earthly state" (29). While the Almond children are having a picnic on a hill overlooking Felling and the North Sea, they witness the ceremony, which includes the blowing of the trumpet, the ringing of the bell, and the beating of the boundaries. The practice, explained by the town clerk as dating from before maps were widely available, now includes only a "pretend" beating of the children, accompanied by much false shrieking and genuine laughter. Once the procession moves on, the Almond children eat their picnic food and trace maps of themselves on the ground with a stick.

The idyllic afternoon and the quaint practice take a sinister turn when the children witness a young boy being beaten by his older brother. They rescue the young boy, who identifies himself as Valentine Carr—his name stemming from the fact that he was born on St. Valentine's Day. ("Carr" is a name Almond uses again in *Heaven Eyes*, for one of the orphans, January Carr.) The children do their best to comfort Valentine, while Margaret makes figures out of clay, including some with wings in yet another recurrence of the angel motif that appears throughout these stories. As the day wanes, the children prepare to leave so that they can visit their mother, who is hospitalized because of her severe arthritis. The mother's physical limitations serve as a palpable reminder to the children, and to us as readers, of the clear boundaries of human existence. This theme is echoed in the fate of one of Margaret's clay angels: its surface begins to crumble and one of its wings breaks off. The boundaries of human existence are also evident in the Carr family. When the children return Valentine to his home, his father, angry that the boy's brother has abused and abandoned him, begins yelling at and beating his older son, illustrating the sad age-old truth that violence begets violence. The vicious cycle of child abuse is a theme that will resurface in the Askew family in *Kit's Wilderness*. Both "Beating the Bounds" and "Counting the Stars" emphasize the theme of human limitations, while at the same time depicting a very human desire for transcendence. Both stories focus on the physical aspects of life, but thematically they pave the way for a magical realist perspective that offers hope for transcendence, a perspective that is hinted at in other stories and fully realized in the novels.

Memory and Imagination

The power of memory and imagination in connecting us to those who have been lost through death is a theme that unites many of the stories. "The Angel of Chilside Road," for example, is a brief sketch that focuses on Barbara shortly after her death. The title refers to the fact that a week after the child's death, a neighbor saw Barbara, dressed in white, walking along Chilside Road with her mother. The vision clearly suggests the miraculous, for Barbara had been an invalid and at this point her mother was already wracked with arthritis. Yet in the vision both are walking easily, and a light is radiating from Barbara. The vision is said to have brought great comfort to the Almond children's mother—and indeed to the whole family, for in their dreams they follow "the angel that was seen on Chilside Road that day" (58). Like the angel in *Skellig*, the vision in this story serves to infuse the physical realities of life and death with the promise of the mystical and miraculous. The vision seems to confirm the truth of the inscription on the Almond family tombstone: indeed, the dead "are equal unto the angels" (7).

The reported vision of Barbara as an angel ironically seems more vivid in David's memory than the photographs of Barbara, as described in the sketch "Barbara's Photographs." This is understandable, given that most of Barbara's photographs were removed from the household by some well-meaning person shortly after the child's death. David thinks he remembers a photograph of his sister sitting in the cradle beside the sea, obviously taken during a family outing at the beach. But he admits this memory might be of his sister Mary, not Barbara, for "[m]emory, dream, desire, imagination have mingled through the years" (80). As a result, he knows that he and his family will "remember" Barbara by constantly reinventing her in their minds. The nature of memory is thus like the creative process, providing not a faithful recording of what was but rather an imaginative re-creation of what might have been.

The theme of memory is at the heart of "My Mother's Photographs" as well. In this sketch, David reflects on photographs of his mother, taken before any of her children were born and before she was ravaged by arthritis. The photographs show her to have been beautiful and a gifted dancer. As he gazes at these images of his mother, David wonders if the arthritis was already present in her then, waiting like a secret, insidious force to erupt. He also reflects on how much he and his siblings mirror his mother, serving as living embodiments of her memory. He writes, "We are photographs ourselves. Her image is upon us" (145). Memory here is more internalized and more sure, for after all, David and his brother and sisters have ample images of their mother, both in photographs and in their own minds. But they also have one another to serve as living physical reminders of their mother's image. Each of them, it would seem, reflects their mother in some way.

One of David's more vivid memories of his father is described in "The Time Machine," a story about when his father took him to see the Time Machine at a local traveling carnival. As it turns out, David's father visited this same sideshow attraction when he was a boy. The "machine" itself, of course, turns out to be a hoax. When David volunteers to take a trip in it (with his father's encouragement), he discovers that it is nothing but a shelf containing a few books, including one entitled *The Shape of Things to Come*. The carnival barker's beautiful assistant implies that she will grant David sexual favors if he keeps the secret of the time machine. Like his father before him, David agrees to keep the secret. The experience does, however, prove to be a kind of time machine, connecting father and son in a common experience. Occurring just a year before the father's death, it also provides David with one of his more vivid memories of his dad. Moreover, by taking his son to visit the attraction, the father is able, in a sense, to go back in time to his own childhood and at the same time to see the future in the form of his son.

A companion story (although it appears much later in the book) is the rather intriguingly titled "Buffalo Camel Llama Zebra Ass," a story also about a visit to a traveling carnival. This time, it is the children who go. In fact, by this time, the father has died and the mother is debilitated by arthritis. The title refers to a small menagerie that appears as part of the show. Mary and Margaret begin to imitate the animals in a playful sort of way until a schoolmate's mother scolds them for lowering themselves to the status of beasts. She warns them that if they continue such behavior, they will never see their father in Heaven. Once she is out of carshot, though, the girls call her a pig and a cow. The story ends with an implicit connection between the animals and the Almond children. As if to echo the title, the final sentence of the story presents an alphabetical list of the children's names, ending with David's: "Me" (195). Whereas "The Time Machine" represents a vivid memory David has of his father, this story represents a vivid memory he shares with his sisters and brother. It celebrates the connection to nature and to family while criticizing the rigid moralizing and scare tactics of organized religion.

Journeys Outward and Inward

Family is a central theme in most of these stories, but some of the stories deal more overtly with the adolescent's desire to distance him/herself, at least temporarily, from family ties. For David's sister Mary, that desire is manifested in her attempt to join a traveling street band. "The Fuselier" depicts this attempt and her brothers' and sisters' efforts at retrieving her, as they think all the while about family members they have lost through death. As it turns out, Mary cannot join the band unless her mother can accompany her, which is impossible given the mother's severe arthritis. The others know that, ironically, it is only the mother who can truly understand Mary's fascination with the musical life and her disappointment in being thwarted. In the end, the girls form their own band, much to their mother's delight and encouragement. The story ends with the siblings grown, telling their own children about the day Mary ran off to join the Fuseliers. It seems that even in the desire to break away, there are the seeds of return, for the experience connects Mary even more strongly to her family, both at the time and in the future when the story is recounted again and again.

David's own desire to escape for awhile is seen in the story "Jonadab." Jonadab is the name David's grandfather uses when he means to name an exotic place, "an invented place," a place designed to stop children's questions (81). David is thus delighted when he one day notices the obscure name on a map at school. He immediately determines to go there. When he arrives, he encounters two seemingly wild children (somewhat like those in the play *Wild Girl, Wild Boy*). The girl brandishes a knife, and the boy claims to have seen ghosts and dog children. Menacing at first, the girl and boy eventually accept David, an act they symbolize by the time-honored ritual of cutting thumbs and exchanging blood. Jonadab turns out to be both grotesque and familiar, a bizaare place with even more bizaare people, but people who turn out to constitute simply a different kind of family for David. In the end, of course, David returns to the familiarity of home, but he yearns for the moment to stay in Jonadab and even to journey to "unknown places with these gentle children and their beasts" (96). The story symbolizes one aspect of the adolescent journey toward independence and self-discovery, it confirms the presence of the extraordinary within the ordinary world, and ultimately it affirms the power, and fluidity, of family.

Other stories in *Counting Stars* deal with David's more inner journey toward self-discovery and adult awareness. "Behind the Billboards" is the story of a bully, Stoker, who has been terrorizing David and his friends Mickey, Tash, and Coot. One day, in an attempt to avoid Stoker, the four boys hide between the tall billboards and the wall of a warehouse. While hiding, the other boys tease Coot about having no father, about being, as they say, a "bastard." They know that Coot cries easily, and, much like the bully that is terrorizing all of them, they terrorize Coot. Unable to take any more taunting, Coot leaves the hiding place, apparently willing to risk his chances with Stoker. Indeed, Stoker does spy Coot and begins following him, thus allowing the other boys to escape, at least for the time being. As he heads home, David feels shame at what he and the other boys have done to Coot but also happiness for having escaped Stoker's clutches. The story of bullies is one that recurs in Almond's writing, but the portrayals are not simplistic. As in this story, the nature of bullying is seen as complex, and the capacity to be a bully resides in many people, adults as well as children.

In "Chickens" David is once again the object of bullying. On his way home from his grandfather's house, carrying flowers and a head of lettuce, he is set upon by the Hutchinson brothers, who get angry at him because he ignores them. They crush the flowers and kick the lettuce to pieces. When David's brother, Colin, learns what has happened, he sends David to get another head of luttuce while he goes to talk with the Hutchinsons. To David's surprise, however, Colin makes peace with the brothers and even invites them to go to the grandfather's greenhouse for some uninterrupted fun while the grandfather is at the local pub. Once at the greenhouse, the boys smoke cigarettes and play cards with a deck containing pictures of naked women. David, not quite a boy and not yet a man, is disturbed by the cards, partly because he is afraid that his grandfather will return at any minute and partly because the pornographic images on the cards make him genuinely uncomfortable. When David insists that it is time to go, one of the Hutchinson brothers accuses him of being a chicken. This event, while obviously crude and seemingly insignificant, represents a stage in David's initiation into sexuality and manhood, a theme that is explored more fully in two other stories.

Body and Spirit

Two stories in particular depict David's struggle between sexual desire and spiritual transcendence. "The Subtle Body" is a coming-of-age story about (what appears to be) a first crush and sexual encounter. Significantly, David first sees Theresa, the visiting cousin of a local girl, while attending a Good Friday service at church. His friend, Mick Flannery, describes her as "an angel" (98), but, of course, it is the girl's physical allure rather than her spiritual quality that attracts both boys. This is a time in David's life when he is drifting away from the Church, finding more sustenance in the books of the local library than in the teachings of the faith. Specifically, he is drawn to the writings of T. Lobsang Rampa, actually an Irishman masquerading as a Tibetan monk, who advocates transcendence of the body through the power of the imagination. Try as he might, David is unable to achieve such an experience, for he is tied too closely to his familiar physical surroundings. His infatuation with Theresa makes bodily transcendence even more difficult. Yet he discovers, somewhat ironically, that through his awakening sexuality and through physical contact with Theresa, he *is* able to achieve the transcendence that he cannot accomplish through the imagination alone. He comes to realize that together they "can imagine anything" and "go anywhere" (111). In this story neither the Church nor a spiritual alternative prove to be as potent as "the subtle body" itself in transcending the boundaries of ordinary life.

The concluding story of the collection, "Where Your Wings Were," fuses spirituality with physical desire while connecting the past to the present through memory and dreams. This story provides a reprise of the motifs we have seen throughout the book, including, most obviously, the image of the angel. The title refers to the fact that for a long time after Barbara's death, David's mother would place her hand beneath David's shoulder blades and tell him that that is where his wings once were and that one day he would get them back. (This is something that Michael's mother tells him as well in *Skellig*.) At night, David tries to see Barbara in his dreams as an angel in Heaven. As he grows older, however, he says that he "could feel the goodness leaving me" (197) and that, as a result, his prayers to his departed sister seemed empty and ineffectual. His diminishing faith coincides with his developing sexuality, and he begins having a dream of a very sexual angel whose embrace fills him with a fiery pleasure. When he confesses his dreams to the local priest, the old man is outraged. David, however, continues to take pleasure in the dreams, eventually receiving a message from Barbara saying that she is all right. This dream/vision, while undermining the strict teachings of the Church, comforts David and gives him both physical pleasure and spiritual knowledge that one day he too will have his wings back. As the concluding story in the book, "Where Your Wings Were" serves to consolidate the recurring theme of the presence of the wondrous and magical amid the physical and ordinary, and also points to themes that will emerge in the novels: magic, memory, death, and the power of the creative imagination.

Individual and Society

Only three of the stories in *Counting Stars* focus on characters who are not part of the Almond family. Each of these stories presents a portrait of a marginalized character, someone who is eccentric, mentally challenged, mute, persecuted, exploited, lost in the past, and/or trapped in his or her own interior worlds. Each of these characters, however, is part of David's education about life, adulthood, the community, and the Church. The main character in "The Baby" is Miss Golightly, a seamstress who made David's clothes when he was a boy. With her silver earrings and thin mustache, she seems exotic to the children and is rumored, according to her nephew Kev, to be a witch. David is fond of her, though, even when her needlework is no longer very reliable. He enjoys looking at the faded photographs on her walls, depicting scenes of Felling from years before. On one Remembrance Day, Miss Golightly shows David a picture of a dark-haired soldier, a young man who was once her lover before he was lost in the war. Whether he was killed in battle or died of disease is unclear, for when David asks her what happened to him, her response is one simple word: "Death" (48). Miss Golightly then shows David a fetus in a jar, and tells him that the child would have been her boy, "like you are," she says (49). Earlier, the eleven-year-old David has looked at himself in the mirror and seen a baby, a boy, and the likeness of her parents all bound up in his image. The way the past is realized in the present—and in the future—is emphasized both in David's growth and maturation and in Miss Golightly's arrested development. She is stuck in time, living a life as faded as that in her photographs, suspended like her stillborn child in the jar. When Miss Golightly dies, her nephew discovers the fetus and shows it to David, who of course already knows about it. In a final act of homage to Miss Golightly, David takes the fetus from Kev, baptizes it so that it will not be condemned to Limbo, and buries it. As he baptizes the fetus, he names it "Anthony," giving him his father's name and the name Miss Golightly had intended for him had he lived. David's action shows both his belief in the teachings of the Church (at this time) and his desire to remedy a situation that had seemed so filled with pathos. This desire is manifested further in what he does when he gets home: he begins writing the story of Miss Golightly, her soldier, and her baby. The seed of this story, we may assume, grew into the story we see before us. This attempt to rectify the past through the creative process is one that we see in Almond's novels as well, most obviously in his creating an angel in *Skellig* to rescue a baby that is critically ill. It does not seem far-fetched to suggest that in writing the novel, Almond was working out his own grief and sense of helplessness over his baby sister, Barbara's, untimely death. In the novel, Almond is able to imagine a different outcome, one in which the mystical and miraculous is discovered amid the natural world.

But, if "The Baby" appears to confirm the possibility of the miraculous in everyday life, the two other stories that focus on eccentric characters question that belief. "Loosa Fine," for example, tells the story of a mentally challenged girl, a young woman who, like Barbara, will always be a little girl not because her development is arrested by death but because of her physical and mental limitations. In the story Loosa, whose name is a corruption of "Louisa," a name the girl cannot pronounce properly, is taken to Lourdes by the local parish so that she may benefit from bathing in the healing waters. While there, she claims to receive messages from the Virgin Mary telling her that she is lovely and revealing other secrets to her. On this pilgrimage, Loosa is cared for by a member of a neighboring parish, a woman named Doreen, who is described at one point as the girl's guardian angel.

But Doreen turns out to be more demon than angel, exploiting Loosa by hiring her out to boys for sex. Even Loosa's visions are called into question by some of the witnesses who think their source is Hell rather than Heaven. The story grapples with the question of what Loosa really is: child or adult, innocent victim or instrument of evil. Ultimately, Loosa becomes pregnant and is taken from her mother by the Church and sent to live in a convent where the nuns will take care of her and find a good home for her baby. The portrayal of the Church and its devout followers in the story is in many ways as complex and contradictory as the portrayal of Loosa herself. In one sense, the Church is compassionate, trying to secure a miracle for the girl and then providing care for her after she becomes pregnant. At the same time, the Church seems as willing to exploit Loosa for its own advantage as does Doreen, herself a member of the Church if not a devout follower of its teachings. In taking Loosa to Lourdes, what did the members of the local parish hope to achieve? A miracle perhaps, or at least some sort of mystical experience that would confirm the Church's teachings about the possibilities of transcending the physical boundaries of life. In the end, though, Loosa's experience both raises the possibility of such transcendence and calls into question that possibility. As in "Counting the Stars," the efficacy of the Church comes under scrutiny with questions raised but no satisfactory conclusion drawn at the end of the story.

Similarly, "Jack Law" questions the rigid disciplinary code of church and school, as exemplified by the sadistic headmistress, Miss Sloane. Jack Law is another of Almond's marginalized characters. A ghostly presence in the town for many years, someone we would now call "homeless," he wanders the town with a faraway look in his eyes, never speaking a word. The story of what happened to Jack to make him that way is told to David by Carmel Bright, a friend of David's grandmother and a former schoolmate of Jack's. It seems that when Jack, who had always been "slow" (179), had trouble learning his catechism, he was forced by the headmistress to stand outside in frigid weather. Because Jack's family was poor, the boy was wearing nothing but rags. After this ordeal, Jack lost the ability to speak. According to Carmel Bright, in spite of this great injustice, nothing was ever done to the headmistress. The story ends on what may be a sardonic note, with Carmel saying that such things would not be allowed to happen "in these days of enlightenment and loss of faith" (188). Her statement does not quite ring true, though, and one is left wondering—along with David, it would seem—whether the Church has been purged of such abusers and/or whether the Church's influence has indeed waned. If the Church's teachings and rituals offer comfort and hope in "The Baby" and "The Angel of Chilside Road," they seem at best ineffectual and at worst sinister in "Loosa Fine" and "Jack Law." Taken together, though, these four stories portray in a realistic, complex way the internal struggle of a sensitive adolescent whose growing awareness causes him to question the belief system in which he has been indoctrinated. These stories indicate both a desire to renounce the Church's methods and teachings and a yearning to embrace its promise of hope and spiritual transcendence.

Taken together, the stories in *Counting Stars* constitute a rich tapestry of Almond's life experiences, chronicling his growth and development as an adolescent. The dominant themes that emerge indicate the oppositional struggles in young David's psyche: family and community versus alienation, Church dogma versus natural morality, spiritual transcendence versus physical desire, memory as historical record versus memory as creative act, fiction versus truth. Many of these themes will resurface in the novels, to be explored in more depth. Although I have stated these themes as a series of oppositions here, in reality Almond presents them—both in *Counting Stars* and in his novels—not as mutually exclusive, but rather as more complex dualities often involving both terms in the lives and minds of his protagonists. Growing up, Almond suggests, involves dealing with such multifarious issues in a process that proves to be as exhilarating, complicated, and ultimately unfathomable as counting the stars.

Notes

1. The four stories from *Counting Stars* are, in this order, "The Middle of the World," "Counting the Stars," "The Subtle Body," and "Where Your Wings Were." The middle story in the volume is "The Built-up Sole," about a curmudgeonly local barber with one leg shorter than the other—hence his need to have a built-up sole on one of his shoes. An object of pity and ridicule, he is tormented by some of the teenaged boys of the town, including the narrator

(presumably David). As an outcast and victim of persecution, he has much in common with Loosa Fine, Jack Law, and Miss Golightly in *Counting Stars*.

2. Kathleen Odean, "Mystic Man," *School Library Journal* 47.4 (2001): 48–52, *WilsonSelectPlus*, H. W. Wilson, online, 1 June 2003.

3. Erica Wagner, "Vivid Bedtime Stories for Young and Old Alike," rev. of *Counting Stars*, by David Almond, *The Times* [London] 15 November 2000, *Lexis-Nexis*, online, 4 June 2003.

4. Hazel Rochman, rev. of *Counting Stars*, by David Almond, *Booklist* 98.11 (2002), *Children's Literature Reviews*, *Children's Literature Comprehensive Database*, online, 29 May 2003.

5. Rev. of *Counting Stars*, by David Almond, *Kirkus Reviews* 70.6 (2002), *Children's Literature Reviews*, *Children's Literature Comprehensive Database*, online, 29 May 2003.

6. Elizabeth Bush, rev. of *Counting Stars*, by David Almond, *Bulletin of the Center for Children's Books* 55.7 (2002), *Children's Literature Reviews*, *Children's Literature Comprehensive Database*, Oneline, 29 May 2003.

7. Gregory Maguire, rev. of *Counting Stars*, by David Almond, *Horn Book* 78.2 (2002): 207–8.

8. Philip Pullman, "Spellbinding Realism," rev. of *Counting Stars*, by David Almond, *Guardian Unlimited* 28 September 2000, online, 1 September 2005, http://books.guardian.co.uk/booksareforever/story/0,,373653,00.html.

9. William McLoughlin, rev. of *Counting Stars*, by David Almond, *School Library Journal* 48.3 (2002): 225.

10. Sherrie Williams, rev. of *Counting Stars*, by David Almond, VOYA, 25.3 (2002), *Children's Literature Reviews*, *Children's Literature Comprehensive Database*, online, 29 May 2003.

11. The concept of polyphony derives from the work of Mikhail Bakhtin, who argues that polyphonic narratives contain different, and often competing, voices, instead of a single narrative voice. See *The Dialogic Imagination: Four Essays*, ed. Michael Holquist, trans. Caryl Emerson and Michael Holquist (Austin, TX: University of Texas Press, 1981). Rosemary Ross Johnston discusses Almond's use of heteroglossia, another Bakhtinian concept closely related to polyphony, in his play *Wild Girl, Wild Boy*. See "Carnivals, the Carnivalesque, *The Magic Puddin'*, and David Almond's *Wild Girl, Wild Boy*: Toward a Theorizing of Children's Plays," *Children's Literature in Education* 34.2 (2003): 141.

CHAPTER THREE

~

Extraordinary Beings: *Skellig*, Novel and Play

Skellig, Almond's first true work for young adults, tells the story of Michael, a sensitive boy, and his friend Mina, who discover an angelic creature living in Michael's family's garage. The novel's pervasive concern with how the magical is manifested in everyday life places it squarely within the literary tradition known as "magical realism." In its intertextuality as well as its focus on the dream-like state between life and death and between childhood and adulthood, the novel exemplifies a concern with that "liminal territory" characteristic of so much magical realist fiction.[1] The infusion of the magical in everyday life—and the special ability of young people to recognize that—is a major theme of *Skellig*. To explore the presence of the extraordinary in the ordinary world, Almond weaves a narrative fabric made up of rich intertextual references and vivid dream imagery. The psychological terrain of the novel is therefore what may be described as a "magical realist dreamscape," a surreal territory in which the distinction between reality and dreams and between the ordinary and the magical are blurred. As Michael's friend Mina wisely comments at one point, "'Truth and dreams are always getting muddled'" (52). It is within this liminal territory that Michael and Mina learn to recognize the presence of the extraordinary in everyday life and, moreover, to recognize the presence of the extraordinary within themselves.

There are two interrelated stories in *Skellig*. One is the story of how Michael discovers an angel living in his family's garage, how he and his friend Mina help restore the angel to health, and how the angel helps them to recognize the possibility of magic in the world. The other story involves Michael's baby sister, who is seriously ill. Michael's feelings of helplessness in relation to his sister are transformed into a desire to help Skellig, which he does by bringing him food and aspirin and eventually moving him out of the garage and into the attic of an empty house. When Skellig is restored to health, he flies away, but before he does, he visits Michael's baby sister in the hospital and heals her. In effect, Michael has helped to heal his baby sister through his and Mina's ministrations to Skellig.

The novel was widely reviewed and well received by critics and the public alike. Ilene Cooper, reviewing the novel for *Booklist*, wrote that "[s]ome of the writing takes one's breath away, especially the scenes in which Almond, without flinching, describes the beauty and the horror that is Skellig."[2] The reviewer for *Kirkus* praised Almond for creating "a powerful, atmospheric story," for "delineating characters with brilliant economy," and for mixing "the marvelous and the everyday . . . in haunting, memorable ways."[3] Claire Rosser called the novel "a profound book" that encourages us to experience the wonder of "the things right in front of all of us each moment."[4] And Perri Klass, writing in *The New York Times Book Review*, applauded Almond's "cheerful interweaving of everyday detail," his "simple but poetic language," and his achievement in transcending the typical young adult fare to offer "a story about worlds enlarging and the hope of scattering death."[5] To be sure, the combination of fantasy and realism did not work for every reviewer. Elizabeth Bush, for instance, complained that "[o]nce Skellig's benign nature is revealed . . . there's simply not enough drama in the bug/owl/man plot to sustain the suspense."[6] In general, though, most critics felt that *Skellig* was a remarkable first novel, and the book went on to receive several prestigious awards. It was the Carnegie Medal winner and the Whitbread Children's Book of the Year Award winner in the United Kingdom, and in the United States it was named a Michael L. Printz Honor Book. Clearly, to many reviewers and award committees, a fresh new voice had emerged on the scene of young adult literature.

Magical Realism

Almond's debt to magical realism, and especially to Gabriel García Márquez, is evident in the novel's central conceit.[7] The story of an extraordinary, angelic being who turns up in a most ordinary place recalls García Márquez's 1968 story "A Very Old Man with Enormous Wings," subtitled "A Tale for Children." In this story, a young couple, with a very sick baby, discover an old man with tattered wings lying in a puddle of mud outside their home. After taking the old man in, the couple soon discover, to their great delight, that the baby's health has been restored. Not sure what to do with the angel, the couple places him in a cage and then solicit the advice of neighbors and the local priest. Word spreads and soon people are coming from miles around to gawk at the angel. However, the crowd's curiosity quickly wanes, and soon they are in pursuit of another, more dramatic spectacle. The angel, having by now regained his strength, flies away, much to the relief of the young couple who have grown tired of caring for him.

Examining the similarities and the differences between García Márquez's story and Almond's novel can help to illuminate more clearly Almond's distinctive use of magical realism for his particular purposes. The similarities between the story and the novel are fairly obvious but instructive nonetheless. Michael discovers a decrepit angel-like creature living in the decaying garage at his family's new house, just as the young couple of García Márquez's story discovers a decrepit old man with wings lying in a mud puddle outside of their home. There is an indication in both works that these angels may actually be angels of death. For one thing, they both initially appear to be close to death themselves. The old man of the story is frail, bald, and almost toothless. Similarly, Skellig, when Michael first discovers him, is frail and racked with arthritis. Moreover, both characters are associated with images of death. García Márquez's angel is described as having "buzzard wings" that are "dirty and half-plucked."[8] Skellig is described as being covered with dust, cobwebs, and dead bluebottle flies. In the story, a neighbor, who has been summoned by the young couple, surmises that the angel had come for the sick baby but got blown off course by the storm. It is equally likely that Skellig is waiting in the garage to take Michael's ill baby sister. Furthermore,

Skellig has been in the garage for some time, including the time during the previous owner's sickness and death. Yet, if both angels are intended to be angels of death, they, in fact, are transformed into angels of healing: the young couple's baby recovers from a high fever, and Michael's sister comes through heart surgery safely. In each case, it seems that the angel's original purpose changes because of the kindness shown him by the story's protagonists. The healing of each child may, of course, be explained in a variety of ways, not all of which involve miraculous intervention. Nevertheless, it seems fair to claim that *if* the healings are miraculous, they almost certainly occur, indirectly, through human agency. In the end, both angels regain their strength and fly away.

There are some significant differences, too, in the effects to which the two writers employ magical realism. For one thing, García Márquez's angel is very much a public figure throughout the story, while Almond's angel is very much private, known only to Michael and Mina. It never seems to occur to Pelayo and Elisenda to keep the existence of their angel a secret. On the contrary, they invite their neighbors along with the local priest, and they are delighted to discover that people will pay to see the angel. As a result, the angel becomes a sideshow attraction, much like "a circus animal."[9] He suffers further humiliation when the priest decides that he looks too human to be a supernatural being, and then darkly adds that the devil is capable of using such trickery. The ultimate insult comes when the crowds abandon the angel in search of greater novelty: a new and better carnival attraction arrives in the form of a woman who has been transformed into a spider because of disobeying her parents. When the angel finally flies away, the young couple is happy to be rid of what had become to them an annoyance.

Skellig's treatment at the hands of Michael and Mina stands in sharp contrast to the treatment García Márquez's angel receives. They never reveal his existence to anyone else, although they have the opportunity on several occasions to tell their parents about him. They seem to know instinctively that the only way to save him is to protect the secret of his existence. In addition, they care for him, bringing him food and medicine, and they eventually move him into the attic of Mina's grandfather's now empty house. Thanks to the ministrations of Michael and

Mina and the attic owls, Skellig not only survives but is transformed into a strong, beautiful creature who is able to fly away. The children are not happy to see him go, but they are pleased that he is well again and that, wherever he goes, someone else might have the good fortune of discovering him.

The universe of Almond's novel, much like that of García Márquez's story, is one in which the extraordinary is always palpably present behind the mundane, but, unlike the story, Almond's novel suggests that only a few are gifted with the ability to perceive that presence. Michael and Mina have this gift, and, through their interactions with Skellig as well as their interactions with each other, they come to recognize the presence of the marvelous in their lives and within themselves. García Márquez's purpose is to critique the foibles of society by showing how adults mistreat an angelic visitor, and his subtitle, "A Tale for Children," surely should be taken with a grain of salt. Almond's purpose is quite different. He focuses on two extraordinary adolescents, and uses Skellig as a device for exploring and affirming their capacity for discernment, compassion, and kindness.

William Blake

The theme of discernment, i.e., the ability to recognize the magical amidst the real, is reinforced through numerous allusions to William Blake, which serve to emphasize the visionary ability of the two main characters while also echoing the mysterious, magical nature of Skellig himself. As Mina's mother explains when she sees her daughter's painting of a man with wings: "[It is the] kind of thing William Blake saw. He said we were surrounded by angels and spirits. We must just open our eyes a little wider, look a little harder" (131). She then shows Michael some of Blake's drawings of the "winged beings [Blake] saw in his little home in London," and comments, "Maybe we could all see such beings, if only we knew how to" (132). Michael and Mina, of course, *do* know how to, and in that sense they both share Blake's capacity for discernment.

Mina, however, is the one with whom the Blake references are most closely connected. She often sings or quotes Blake's verses, and it is she who introduces Michael to Blake's poetry. Like Blake, Mina is a talented illustrator, and like Blake, she is an outsider, strongly individualistic, set apart from the other children in the community because she is homeschooled. She even resembles Blake in appearance: at one point Michael notes that Blake was small and red-headed, just like Mina. It is even possible, given Mina's mother's fondness for Blake, that she named her daughter after the poet, "Mina" being short for "Wilhelmina," a feminized version of "William."[10]

Most of the poems referenced in the novel come from Blake's illuminated book *Songs of Innocence and of Experience*. As the title suggests, these poems explore the tensions inherent in the dichotomy between innocence and experience, between childhood and adulthood. Blake's poetry is redolent with images and themes that are echoed in the novel, including the constraints of school, the association of birds with the innocence and vulnerability of children, the presence of guardian angels in the world, the magical and revelatory power of dreams, and the stifling effects that becoming an adult has on one's ability to perceive the extraordinary in the world.

Mina is homeschooled, and she clearly enjoys ridiculing what she imagines to be the rigidity and absurdities of Michael's more formal schooling. When she discovers that a red sticker on one of his schoolbooks denotes reading level, she asks sarcastically whether Blake's poem "The Tyger"—"'Tyger! Tyger! burning bright / In the forests of the night'"—would be considered appropriate for the best or the worst readers (90). Later, she makes fun of his schoolmates by quoting from Blake's "English Encouragement of Art" (which does not appear in *Songs of Innocence and of Experience*): "'Thank God I was never sent to school, / To be flog'd into following the style of a Fool'" (109). Like Blake, Mina takes a bleak view of the overly rigid classroom that constricts young minds by emphasizing the mundane and thus squelching children's ability to see the magic of the everyday world. An excerpt from Blake's "The School-Boy" hangs over Mina's bed: "'How can a bird that is born for joy / Sit in a cage and sing?'" (50). And, in commenting on the young birds outside her window, Mina notes that they will learn to fly without the necessity of classroom training. She later reads to Michael from the same poem:

> But to go to school in a summer morn,
> O! it drives all joy away;

> Under a cruel eye outworn,
> The little ones spend the day
> In sighing and dismay. (59)

The image of a caged bird serves as an apt metaphor for the hapless child's situation among the excessive regimentation of school.

It is tempting to see Mina's comments as reflecting Almond's own attitude, for, after all, he has acknowledged in interviews that as a child he loved reading but disliked school and as an adult he found only limited satisfaction in teaching.[11] However, the narrative actually presents a more complex view. Yes, there is an implied criticism of reading-level stickers on books and simplistic fill-in-the-blank worksheets. At the same time, though, the novel presents sympathetic portraits of some teachers, including Mrs. Dando, who brings Michael his homework when he has to miss school, and Miss Clarts, who encourages Michael in his story writing. And Michael himself seems to like at least some parts of school. When Mina makes derisive comments about school, he protests that she does not know what she is talking about. In fact, more than once he is brought almost to the point of tears by her sarcasm. The narrative effectively presents a nuanced, balanced view of formal schooling, suggesting that it can be stifling at times and inspiring at others. Paradoxically, by using Blake's poems, which admittedly reflect only one viewpoint, Almond is able to present his own multifaceted view.

As several of his poems attest, a favorite conceit of Blake's was the association of birds with the freedom and innocence of children, and in the novel this association proves to be a useful metaphor for Almond as well. In the poem "Night," another favorite of Mina and her mother, an implicit connection is made between sleeping birds and sleeping children:

> The sun descending in the west.
> The evening star does shine.
> The birds are silent in their nest,
> And I must seek for mine . . . (137)

Although these are the only lines from "Night" quoted in the novel, the curious reader who seeks out the entire poem will find that it goes on to describe the presence of angels in the world, watching over the innocent and vulnerable:

> Unseen they pour blessing,
> And joy without ceasing,
> On each bud and blossom,
> And each sleeping bosom.[12]

The poem deftly connects the spiritual realm with the natural world, depicting angels as "look[ing] into every thoughtless nest / Where birds are covered warm."[13] These images of birds and angels resonate with recurring images in the novel: Skellig himself seems both avian and angelic, while Mina, Michael, and Michael's baby sister are all compared to both birds and angels.

The capacity for discerning the presence of the magical amidst the real, while more clearly associated with children, is also possible for adults. The fact that Mina's mother is intimately familiar with Blake's poems, for example, suggests that she still has some appreciation for the presence of the magical within the world, and undoubtedly she is the one who introduced Blake's poetry to Mina and helped foster her daughter's appreciation for the extraordinary. This gift of discernment, however, is in danger of being stifled and even eradicated by the process of becoming an adult. In one scene, Mina's mother sings Blake's poem "The Angel," which describes a dream about an angel visitation. In the poem, the speaker dreams of being a "maiden Queen" who is guarded by an "Angel mild" (132, 133). The speaker in the poem goes on to say, though, that, because she hid her joy from the angel, the angel flew away. Later, when the angel returned, the speaker as an adult had developed such fierce defense mechanisms that the angel was rendered ineffectual:

> Soon my Angel came again:
> I was arm'd, he came in vain:
> For the time of youth was fled
> And grey hairs were on my head.[14]

The poem suggests that it is the young who have the unique ability to recognize the presence of angels in the world, and that most adults lose this power of discernment. The reference to this poem within the text of the novel makes for a bittersweet effect, raising the question of whether Michael and Mina might one day lose their ability to recognize their angel. The poem serves as an admonition that this could happen, and indeed does happen to many children. At the same time, the novel offers hope that adults—at least some adults, like Mina's mother—can maintain this appreciation for the magical.

The novel ends on a hopeful note, with the naming of Michael's baby sister after she has come home from the hospital. Several names are considered, but the one they finally choose is "Joy." This recalls Blake's poem "Infant, Joy" (not quoted in the novel), which tells of a baby only two days old who exclaims, "Joy is my name."[15] The color illustration that Blake designed to accompany the poem depicts a mother with a baby on her lap being watched over by an angel, who herself appears to be a child. All three are cradled within the petals of an enormous red flower. The poem and the illustration bring together several of the dominant images that appear in *Songs of Innocence and of Experience* and in *Skellig* as well, serving to emphasize the close connection between angels and children. If it is possible that Michael and Mina will lose their capacity for discernment as they become adults, the novel at least suggests that such a capacity is continually renewed in every newborn child.

Dreams

Both of Blake's poems "Night" and "The Angel" depict the revelatory power of dreams to heighten one's awareness of the supernatural within the natural world. Similarly, *Skellig* depicts the work of dreams, either actual dreams or dream-like states, as facilitating discernment of the marvelous. These dreams employ imagery much like that of Blake's poems, including birds, angels, and threatening or ineffectual adults. Most of the dreams reported in the novel are Michael's, and typically they function to make manifest his feelings of fear and powerlessness related to his sister's illness as well as his impressions of the doctors, who seem to him more harmful than helpful. After first discovering Skellig in the garage, and before he even knows Skellig's name, he dreams that the strange man covered with cobwebs and dead flies comes to his room and asks him, "What do you want?" (10). Upon waking, Michael questions whether he really saw Skellig at all or whether it was only a dream. As he lies there in the dark, he hears the baby's breathing, "cracked and hissy" (10), much like the sound of Skellig's voice. This dream paradoxically reinforces and calls into question the encounter Michael has had with Skellig earlier in the day: was there someone in the garage, or did Michael only imagine it? This dream also connects Skellig with the baby, bringing Skellig into Michael's awareness just as he is waking up to his sister's raspy breathing. This connection, introduced here almost subconsciously, is elaborated as the novel progresses and Michael's awareness grows.

Michael has an equally vivid dream after meeting Mina for the first time. She has shown him her sketchbook filled with drawings of various kinds of birds. Alluding to the power of the creative imagination, another recurring theme in the novel, she tells Michael that "[d]rawing makes you look at the world more closely. It helps you to see what you're looking at more clearly" (26). That night Michael dreams that the baby is in the blackbird's nest in Mina's garden. The baby is fed by the blackbird until she becomes strong enough to fly away. In the dream, Mina sketches the baby and warns Michael not to get too close to the nest because he represents danger. Upon waking, Michael hears the baby crying and the birds outside singing. This dream and its immediate aftermath forge a connection in Michael's mind between the vulnerability of his sister and that of baby birds. It also indicates that he is already aware of and respectful of Mina's powers of discernment. Within the dream, Michael's powerlessness to help the baby and his fearful concern for her well-being are transformed in such a way that he sees himself as a threat to the baby's safety. His immediate reaction is to get out of bed and take some aspirin to Skellig. It is as if, because he feels powerless to help the baby, he compensates by helping the strange creature living in his garage, who, he senses, is intimately connected with the child.

Later Michael dreams that both he and the baby are in the blackbird's nest and that two doctors are beneath the tree trying to coax the baby out of the nest. One of the doctors is Dr. MacNabola, the surgeon and arthritis specialist that Michael met when visiting his sister in the hospital, and the other is the baby's doctor, the one Michael calls Dr.

Death. In the dream, the doctors have laid out a table with saws and needles, presumably for treating the baby, although, as Michael has learned in the hospital, these are the instruments used to treat arthritic patients and therefore would seem to be more appropriate for Skellig than for the baby. Here again we see a conflation of Skellig and the child. The doctors are urging the baby to fly out of the nest even though her wings are not fully developed. Michael tries to reach out to save her, but he discovers that he cannot move because his bones are calcified. Again, we see Michael's fear and concern for his sister's well-being. He is no longer a threat, but he is still powerless to help her. This dream also reveals Michael's distrust of the medical establishment, a formidable institution of adult society that represents to Michael the most immediate threat to his sister. Concerning Dr. Death, Michael instinctively knows that "[w]ings [will] never rise at his back" (123).

Significantly, Michael's dream occurs shortly after Michael and Mina have convinced Skellig to let them help him. Michael's fears, as manifested in the dream, are clearly related to his concern for his sister's well-being, but they may also reflect his anxiety, perhaps subconscious, over his and Mina's power to help—or perhaps inadvertently harm—Skellig. Michael also recognizes something in Skellig that causes him to implore Skellig to "'think about the baby . . . to think about her getting better'" (56). This request, along with Michael's and Mina's ministrations, results in Skellig visiting the baby in her hospital room on the night before she is scheduled to have surgery and acting as her guardian angel to bring her safely through the operation. By helping Skellig, Michael is able, with Mina's assistance, indirectly to help the baby. In contrast to the feelings of paralysis he experiences in his dreams, in real life he is able to act decisively—even before he is fully aware of Skellig's true nature.

Another type of dream evident in the novel is the waking dream, a surreal, liminal state between sleeping and waking, between the imaginary and the real. This is the kind of dream Mina refers to when she comes to get Michael so that the two of them can move Skelling into the owl house, the currently empty house that was once Mina's grandfather's house. She asks, "'We're not dreaming this?'" to which Michael replies, "'We're not dreaming it'" (83). Later, after moving Skellig into the attic of the owl house, Michael says that he "imagined that this was a dream . . . that anything was possible in a dream" (86). These particular waking dreams reflect the children's growing sense of wonder as they become increasingly aware of Skellig's extraordinary nature.

Two waking dreams in particular play a pivotal role in the children's recognition of who and what Skellig really is. In one scene, which takes place in the attic of the owl house, Michael and Mina slowly perform a trance-like dance with Skellig, who is stronger now because Michael and Mina have been caring for him and the owls have been feeding him. As Skellig grasps Michael's and Mina's hands, the three of them begin to walk slowly in a circle, their faces made alternately dark and light as they step in and out of the moonbeams coming through the window. Michael's feet no longer touch the floor, he sees "ghostly wings" (120) rising at Mina's back, and he feels similar wings rising from his own back. Later, when confronted by Michael's father, who has been frantically searching for the children, they tell him that they have been sleepwalking. Their statement, of course, is a fabrication, an avoidance, but it does reflect the dream-like quality of what they have just experienced. Through this waking dream they come to understand more fully that not only is Skellig an extraordinary being, but they are extraordinary beings as well with a capacity for sprouting wings.

The other waking dream that plays a pivotal role in the children's understanding is not experienced by them directly but is instead reported to them by Michael's mother. The night before the baby's surgery, when Michael's mother was staying with her in the hospital, she says that she dreamed—although she felt wide awake—that a tall, dirty man with kind eyes came into the room, picked up the baby, and began dancing with her. While they were dancing, gossamer wings rose from the baby's back. Afterwards, Michael's mother says that she herself "'slept like a log'" and that intuitively she knew that the baby "'was going to be all right'" (160). The operation is a success, and soon thereafter, Skellig disappears, his work apparently done. Michael's mother's waking dream suggests that Skellig has imparted some kind of magical healing to the baby, most likely in gratitude for the care Michael and Mina have given him.

This dream is pivotal in another sense, as well, suggesting that Michael's mother, much like Mina's mother, has retained some capacity for discerning the presence of the extraordinary in the world. Earlier Michael and Mina have avoided revealing anything to their parents about Skellig's existence. When Mina's mother sees her daughter's sketch of a man with wings and comments on its resemblance to Blake's drawings, Mina has an opportunity to confide in her mother, but instead she chooses to remain silent. Similarly, Michael and Mina tell Michael's father that they have been sleepwalking, when, in fact, they have been visiting Skellig in the owl house. Later, when Michael's mother reveals her "dream" about a man with wings appearing in the baby's hospital room, Michael, of course, knows immediately who the visitor was, but he keeps this information to himself, sharing the news only with Mina. Mina's response is, predictably, to whisper her favorite word: "'Extraordinary'" (163). Michael's and Mina's secretiveness about Skellig may suggest that they have little confidence in their parents' capacity for discernment and wonder, or it may indicate their desire to protect Skellig from a fate similar to that of García Márquez's angel. However, Michael's mother's vision as well as Mina's mother's deep appreciation for Blake suggest that, if these adults are not gifted with the same powers of discernment as their children, they at least have retained some capacity for sensing the wonder and magic inherent in the world.

There is hope also that, as they grow into adulthood, Michael and Mina will retain this capacity as well, perhaps to an even greater extent than their mothers. For now, Michael and Mina are situated in that liminal territory between innocence and experience, between childhood and adulthood. They already possess an inherent magical realist sensibility, but it is through their interactions with Skellig that they are able to realize their true potential. Mina more than once describes Skellig as "extraordinary," and she recognizes the same trait in Michael and herself, whispering to him at one point, "'We are extraordinary'" (99). Michael says, "I stared back. I didn't blink. It was like she was calling Skellig out from somewhere deep inside me" (99). Indeed, Almond's novel suggests, through its use of magical realism, Blake's poetry, and dream imagery, that its adolescent characters are as unique and extraordinary as the enigmatic being who serves as the title character. Ultimately, it is Michael's and Mina's kindness and compassion and their willingness to help Skellig that allow them to realize their extraordinary potential. Before he leaves them, Skellig says to them: "'Pair of angels. . . . That's what you are'"

(167). And when Michael asks him, finally, what he is, he replies: "Something like you, something like a beast, something like a bird, something like an angel" (167). Through their compassionate interactions with Skellig, Michael and Mina not only gain a deeper appreciation for the presence of the extraordinary in the everyday world, but also come to recognize the presence of the extraordinary within themselves, a pivotal recognition that ultimately allows them to soar.

The Play

In November 2003, a theatrical version of *Skellig* was mounted at the Young Vic Theatre in London under the direction of Trevor Nunn with David Threlfall playing the part of Skellig. This was not Almond's first foray into the theater. In February 2001, his play *Wild Girl, Wild Boy* had been produced at the Lyric Theatre, Hammersmith, London. (Because of that play's thematic connection with *Secret Heart*, it will be discussed in chapter 6.) The director Nunn is the one who asked Almond to write the script, after he himself became enchanted with the novel's mixture of the ordinary and the extraordinary: "'The story is magical, poetic, mythic and moving, but, curiously, it's also everyday, real, contemporary and nothing at all like fairy tales.'"[16]

Almond has said that writing for theater is both similar to and different from writing stories and novels. Plays are conceived and first drafts written in the kind of solitude one experiences when writing fiction. But the words on the page have a different look to them: "Dialogue, names, skimpy stage directions, and that's all. The space around the words is for the director, the actors and the designer to fill."[17] A play, therefore, has less "fixity" than a work of fiction and it continues to evolve as it goes into rehearsal, with the director serving as both editor and interpreter.[18] He has also said that part of the appeal of writing plays is to make another sort of connection with the way children respond to narrative: "When children read stories, their first impulse is to act them out."[19]

The play was successful at the box office and was generally well received by critics. John Gross, writing for *The Sunday Telegraph*, said that the production "does full justice to [the] material: the result is . . . at once down to earth and unearthly."[20] Benedict Nightingale, critic for

The Times, was equally enchanted, finding the play to be "touching, even exhilarating."[21] Michael Billington praised Trevor Nunn for "allow[ing] magical moments to grow out of collaborative storytelling techniques," but still found the play "marred by occasional touches of macrobiotic earnestness."[22] And Charles Spencer found the songs distracting in a play that was otherwise "harsh and funny and full of turbulent childhood emotion."[23]

The play *Skellig* is very much like the book in that it maintains the basic story line: a young boy, Michael, finds a decrepit man with wings living in his family's garage. He and his friend Mina help the man, who in turn helps heal Michael's baby sister. The same characters, themes, and motifs are evident, including Mina's antagonism to traditional schooling, her fascination with William Blake, and her access to the "Danger house," i.e., her grandfather's old house with the owls in the attic. The children recognize Skellig as an extraordinary being, although they are never quite sure what he really is, and they come to recognize themselves as extraordinary beings as well. What strikes one in reading the text version of the play is the amount of space given over to narration. And, in fact, that is the term used in the script: not "Narrator," but "Narration," emphasizing the process of telling the story rather than the person doing the telling. Since it is unusual for plays (or films) to have so much narration, it is worth pondering why Almond chose that particular device and used it so extensively in *Skellig*. One obvious answer is that the narration allows for the audience to be told what Michael is experiencing without Michael's having to utter the words in what might come across as a contrived way. It also can provide information about the passage of time and actions that have happened off-stage. For instance, at one point we are told that Michael's mother and the baby have returned from the hospital and that the baby seems well. And the narration can also describe atmosphere in ways that would be hard to render on the stage. It can tell us, for example, that birds are fluttering at the window, and that saves the director from having to try to create what might be difficult to produce in a credible form. So, in that sense, the narration serves a very utilitarian purpose, allowing for a minimalist set with few props and set changes. But the amount of narration also foregrounds the act of storytelling. We are aware at all times that we are listening to and watching a story unfold. The emphasis is as much on the process of narration as it is on what is happening on the stage. The narration thus becomes almost a character in the play—or, to put it another way, the characters in the play are more clearly shown as projections of the narration itself. Either way, the device lends a metafictional quality to the play so that the act of watching the play more closely approximates the act of reading. A person viewing *Skellig* will be called upon to engage her/his imagination perhaps more so than with the typical play. The effect, I would argue, is to encourage each member of the audience to help create the play in much the same way a reader helps to bring a book to life. As Almond explains, "Reading is a creative, imaginative act. The reader helps create the book. Each reader creates a different book."[24] The narration opens up that creative space in the viewer's mind, allowing her/him, for example, to imagine what Michael and Mina feel when they put their hands under Skellig's shoulder blades. Such a viewing experience seems appropriate for a play in which the main character himself defies characterization and invites a multiplicity of interpretations. In the way he creates the theatrical experience, Almond, it seems, is encouraging his audience to give flight to their own imaginations.

Notes

1. Lois Parkinson Zamora and Wendy B. Faris, *Magical Realism: Theory, History, Community* (Durham, NC: Duke University Press, 1995) 6.
2. Ilene Cooper, rev. of *Skellig*, by David Almond, *Booklist* 95.11 (1999), *Children's Literature Reviews*, *Children's Literature Comprehensive Database*, online, 29 May 2003.
3. Rev. of *Skellig*, by David Almond, *Kirkus Reviews* 15 December 1998, *Lexis-Nexis*, online, 17 May 2005.
4. Claire Rosser, rev. of *Skellig*, by David Almond, *KLIATT Review* 33.1 (1999), *Children's Literature Reviews*, *Children's Literature Comprehensive Database*, online, 29 May 2003.
5. Perri Klass, rev. of *Skellig*, by David Almond, *New York Times* 6 June 1999, sec. 7: 49.
6. Elizabeth Bush, rev. of *Skellig*, by David Almond, *Bulletin of the Center for Children's Books* 52.7 (1999), *Children's Literature Reviews*, *Children's Literature Comprehensive Database*, online, 29 May 2003.

7. A much longer version of this section was previously published as "Magical Realism and the Child Reader: The Case of David Almond's *Skellig*." *The Looking Glass: An Online Children's Literature Journal* 10.1 (2006). Available at www.the-looking-glass.net/. Used with permission of *The Looking Glass*.

8. Gabriel García Márquez, "A Very Old Man with Enormous Wings: A Tale for Children," trans. by Gregory Rabassa and J. S. Bernstein, *Collected Stories* (New York: Perennial Classics, 1999) 218.

9. Márquez, "A Very Old Man with Enormous Wings," 219.

10. I am indebted to Katherine V. Graham for this insight. See "Still 'Burning Bright': William Blake's Influence on Contemporary Writers for Children," 31st Annual Conference of the Children's Literature Association, Fresno, CA, 10–12 June 2004.

11. Almond caused a brouhaha among English education officials when, in his Carnegie Medal acceptance speech, he criticized schools' undue emphasis on assessment, targets, and scores, and he offered the rather modest proposal that ten percent of the school year should be liberated from the demands of the national curriculum. The education secretary at the time, David Blunkett, called Almond "a blatant elitist" who was "undermin[ing] educational progress." Several letters appeared in *The Times* in support of Almond, and he himself offered an eloquent defense of his position, which was published in *The Sunday Times*. See Dalya Alberge, "Author Brings 'Stifling' School System to Book," *The Times* [London] 15 July 1999, *NewsBank*, online, 1 September 2005; and David Almond, "Give Our Kids a Break," *The Sunday Times* [London] 3 October 1999, *NewsBank*, online, 1 September 2005.

12. William Blake, "Night," *The Complete Poetry and Prose of William Blake*, ed. by David V. Erdman (New York: Anchor Books, 1988).

13. Blake, "Night," *The Complete Poetry and Prose of William Blake*.

14. Blake, "The Angel," *The Complete Poetry and Prose of William Blake*.

15. Blake, "Infant, Joy," *The Complete Poetry and Prose of William Blake*.

16. "A Hit from a Myth," *The Observer* [London] 23 November 2003, *Guardian Unlimited*, online, 1 September 2005, http://observer.guardian.co.uk/review/story/0,6903,1091171,00.html.

17. David Almond, "Afterword," *Wild Girl, Wild Boy: A Play* (London: Hodder Children's Books, 2002) 89.

18. Almond, "Afterword," 88, 90.

19. David Almond, personal interview, 21 April 2005.

20. John Gross, rev. of *Skellig: The Play*, by David Almond, *The Sunday Telegraph* [London] 14 December 2003, *NewsBank*, online, 1 September 2005.

21. Benedict Nightingale, rev. of *Skellig: The Play*, by David Almond, *The Times* [London] 5 December 2003, *NewsBank*, online, 1 September 2005.

22. Michael Billington, "Trevor Nunn's Tetchy Tramp: *Skellig*," rev. of *Skellig: The* Play, by David Almond, *The Guardian* [London] 5 December 2003, *NewsBank*, online, 1 September 2005.

23. Charles Spencer, "To the Heart of a Children's Classic," rev. of *Skellig: The Play*, by David Almond, *The Daily Telegraph* [London] 5 December 2003, *Lexis-Nexis*, online, 1 September 2005.

24. Almond, "Afterword," 88.

CHAPTER FOUR

~

The Game Called Death: *Kit's Wilderness*

The theme of self-creation through artistic endeavor is evident in *Kit's Wilderness*, the story of three 13-year-olds coming of age against the backdrop of a former coal-mining village in northern England. The wilderness of the title refers to the central image of the novel, a geographical and psychological nexus for the narrator and main character, Kit Watson, and his two friends, Allie Keenan and John Askew. Literally, the wilderness is "an empty space between the houses and the river, where the ancient pit, the mine, had been" (5). Metaphorically, the wilderness represents the psychic turmoil out of which each of the main characters is trying to construct an adult identity through creative activity: Kit is a writer, Askew is an illustrator, and Allie is an actress. For all of them, creative activity is a way of making sense of their world and forging a place for themselves within—or, in the case of Allie, outside of—that world. Creativity is also a way for the three main characters to come to an understanding of the reality of death, a key rite of passage for adolescents.[1]

Kit's Wilderness is the story of Kit Watson, who moves with his parents to Stoneygate, a former coal-mining town, to help care for his ailing grandfather. Part of the novel involves Kit's developing a closer relationship with his grandfather as well as dealing with the old man's increasing senility and impending death. Through his grandfather, he comes to understand more about the history of Stoneygate and his family's connections to that place, and he even begins to see the ghosts of children who lived and died there many years ago. Kit also develops friendships with two of the local children, Allie Keenan, an energetic, mischievous girl who cannot wait to leave Stoneygate, and John Askew, an introverted artist whose family name labels him as a troublemaker. Through the connection of their art, Kit and Askew establish a friendship that helps Kit to come to a fuller understanding of his history while helping to save Askew from himself.

Published in 1999 (2000 in the United States), *Kit's Wilderness* was the eagerly awaited follow-up to *Skellig*, and, for most reviewers, it did not disappoint. Erica Wagner, who had admired *Skellig* for Almond's ability "to combine emotional involvement with a real skill for storytelling," felt that *Kit's Wilderness* was "even better" because it exemplified the best kind of writing, that which "defies categories."[2] While Elizabeth Bush saw the novel as primarily a ghost story with a "burden of subplots"[3] and Susan P. Bloom found "the novel's ambitiousness" to be "both commendable and problematic,"[4] most reviewers admired the literary complexity and richness of imagery. Ilene Cooper, writing in *Booklist*, said that Almond had created "a heartbreakingly real world fused with magical realism," and in doing so had succeeded in "knitting dark and light together and suffusing the multilayered plot with an otherworldly glow."[5] The reviewer for the *Cooperative Children's Book Center Choices* called the novel a "riveting masterpiece" that provided "both literary richness and emotional fulfillment."[6] Kathleen Odean, reviewing the novel for *Book*, felt that "this magical, multilayered story of life, death, and rebirth" provided for a "haunting, memorable" reading experience.[7] Ellen Fader, in *School Library Journal*, described the novel as "a highly satisfying literary experience,"[8] while the reviewer for *The Christian Science Monitor* characterized Almond as a "master storyteller" who had created "a tale in which magic and realism blend as seamlessly as fresh-fallen snow."[9] Bette Ammon, writing for *VOYA*, praised Almond for creating a "mysterious, scary, and enormously satisfying book" filled with "nearly unbearable suspense."[10] And Ken Donelson, reviewing the book in *English Journal*, called the novel "a marvelous story about death and art and aging and forgiving" with "a delightful circularity" in its narrative structure.[11] Like *Skellig, Kit's*

Wilderness won several prizes, including the Michael L. Printz Award and the Smarties Book Prize Silver Award.

Creativity, Identity, and Death

Before turning to the novel, let us first consider the relationship of creative activity to identity formation. In "The Contingency of Selfhood," Richard Rorty argues that selfhood is not a fixed entity but rather a constantly evolving process of self-creation, a "performance" of self through a variety of activities, including artistic activities.[12] In constructing his argument, he synthesizes key ideas from Harold Bloom, Friedrich Nietzsche, and Sigmund Freud. From Bloom, Rorty takes the notion that the true poet is one who is able to break free from received metaphors and create a uniquely descriptive language.[13] From Nietzsche, Rorty derives the concept that the self is not some fixed entity to be discovered and expressed, but rather one that is created through the use of language.[14] And from Freud, Rorty takes the idea that self-creation is not limited to poets and artists, but is instead a process undertaken by everyone. Freud saw each life as consisting of a series of "idiosyncratic narratives—case histories, as it were—of our success in self-creation, our ability to break free from an idiosyncratic past."[15] In summary, Rorty explains that

> the conscious need of the strong poet to *demonstrate* that he is not a copy or replica [is] merely a special form of an unconscious need everyone has: the need to come to terms with the blind impress which chance has given him, to make a self for himself by redescribing that impress in terms which are, if only marginally, his own.[16]

The fluidity of identity is one of the major tenets of magical realism, and magical realist texts often depict the merging, changing, and even multiplying of identities.[17] In *Kit's Wilderness* the fluidity of identity is implicitly suggested by several elements. On a literal level, the characters' physical appearance provides an index to the perception of themselves that they want to create. Allie's colorful, theatrical personality is exemplified by her yellow pants and red shoes as well as her lipstick and eye shadow (28). At the climax of the novel, when she searches for Kit and Askew in the old mining pit, she is wearing her silvery costume from the school play. By way of explanation, she says that she put on the costume "for the publicity," for she expects there to be cameras and reporters when she returns to town with the lost boys (205). In contrast, Askew, who is often seen lingering on the edges of the wilderness, is described as a dark figure wearing black jeans, black sneakers, and a black tee shirt with the word "Megadeth" written on it (6). The fact that Kit never describes himself is significant in that it indicates perhaps his lack of a clear sense of self, at least initially. He seems simultaneously attracted to and repelled by both Allie's theatricality and Askew's darkness and obsession with death, but ultimately Kit must create his own identity.

The theme of fluid identity is also suggested by the multiple names given to the main characters. Allie is called various names throughout the novel. Askew, for example, refers to her as "the stupid pretty one" (89, 103), while Kit's grandpa calls her "Fairy Queen" (80) and "the good bad lass" (93). "Miss Perfect" (81) is the name she uses ironically to describe herself when she is pretending to be a well-behaved, well-mannered student. Askew, likewise, is given a variety of names. His actual name is "John," but he is also called "Askew," by Kit; "caveman" (29), "lout" (76), and "brute" (29), by Allie; and "Johnny" (137), by his father. Kit too has several names. He is known as "Christopher" (76) to his teachers and "Kit" to his family. Allie refers to him, somewhat derisively, as "Mr. New Boy" (29), "Mr. Perfect" (39), and "Mr. Butter Wouldn't Melt" (39). Askew calls him "Mr. Resurrection" (65) after Kit emerges from the abandoned coal pit following a round of the game called Death. This plethora of names suggests both the different roles these teens play and the different ways they are perceived by different people. In short, these multiple names imply that these characters do not have discrete, fixed selves but rather they are what Nina Auerbach, in her discussion of child actors in Victorian society and literature, describes as "a troubling kaleidoscope of beings."[18] This "kaleidoscope of beings," I would argue, is troubling to the main characters of *Kit's Wilderness* because it illustrates the power of other people's perceptions over which the main characters have limited control and against which they must define themselves.

Identity for these three characters is also closely connected with the wilderness of the title, the central metaphor of the novel. The wilderness serves as a liminal space, between the town and the river, hidden from the school and the houses. The wilderness is where the key events of the novel occur, and it is the place to which Kit is drawn again and again. In his acceptance speech for the Michael L. Printz Award, David Almond explains the significance of the wilderness:

> Our children need to know . . . that living, achieving, and aspiring are . . . courageous imaginative acts. It's something we often seem to know, but we seem to keep forgetting. We need to keep reminding ourselves and our children: slow down; wander through the wilderness inside yourself. . . . Take the time to dream, take the time to imagine.[19]

In the "Afterword" to his play *Wild Girl, Wild Boy*, Almond further elucidates the wilderness as a metaphor for the creative imagination:

> This is what the writer does: explore the gardens of the mind, crawl through wilderness, emerge with scratched skin and muddied knees accompanied by words and creatures and images that begin to form themselves into the stories that help to keep the world alive.[20]

The wilderness, then, represents inner geography as much as outer landscape. It is the imaginative garden from which acts of self-creation can emerge.

But the wilderness is also closely connected with death, as is evident in the fact that it is where the children play the game called Death, it is where Kit's grandfather collapses after wandering out of the house, and it is where Kit sees the ghost children of Stoneygate huddled along the periphery. Shortly after Kit moves to Stoneygate, his grandfather takes him to visit the St. Thomas's Church cemetery where he shows him the monument to the 117 victims of the 1821 Stoneygate mine disaster, many of them children. With his grandfather's help, Kit traces among the worn engravings on the tombstone the name of his friend, John Askew, as well as his own name, Christopher Watson, both identified as being aged thirteen. Intuitively, Kit realizes how perilous life must have been for a thirteen-year-old working-class boy in Stoneygate in the early nineteenth century. As his grandfather says, young men then knew what fate held in store for them: like their fathers and grandfathers before them, they would go down into the ground, with fear but also a sense of inevitability, to earn their living. But what Kit also encounters here is an intimation of his own mortality, reflected back to him through the fading inscription on an ancient tombstone. Kit's grandfather also tells his grandson the story of Silky, the mischievous ghost boy who was often seen in the coal mines, just at the edge of the miners' vision. Thought to have been trapped in a tunnel collapse many years ago, this shadowy child seems doomed to haunt the mines for eternity. Kit's grandfather, though his memory is slipping away, still dreams of Silky leading him down dark tunnels. Soon, Kit himself begins to dream of Silky and to see other ghost children, the ancient children of Stoneygate, huddled along the periphery of the wilderness.

Portraits of the Artist

For the main characters in *Kit's Wilderness*, artistic creation is a way of achieving self-creation while also confronting the reality of death. At the heart of the novel are three competing "stories," each serving to provide insight into the developing identities of the main characters. One is the ritual game called Death, created by Askew and played by all three of the characters in the abandoned coal mine. In this game, the children sit in a circle while Askew spins a knife on top of a sheet of glass. Whoever the knife is pointing toward when it stops spinning is the person who will "die" that day. To "die" in this game means to lapse into a momentary catatonic state and to remain alone in the dark mine for an hour or more. Askew's creation of and perpetuation of this game demonstrates his obsession with darkness and death, and it represents a grim reenactment of the numerous mine disasters that have occurred in Stoneygate over the years. Roberta Seelinger Trites notes that, while in children's literature death usually represents a separation from the parent, in adolescent literature it represents a personal threat, something that must be understood and accepted as final if one is to mature into adulthood.[21] This threat, I would argue, is especially significant to the adolescent because it represents the potential annihilation of the fragile, developing self. In the novel, the ritual of the game allows Askew—and the other children—to symbolically confront death and gain control over it. Being the leader of the game also gives him power over the other children. As Geraldine Brennan says, "For [Askew], the game is a way to assert the authority that he cannot acquire through a more respectable route because of his family's reputation [as social outcasts]."[22]

The story with which Allie is associated is the stage adaptation of Hans Christian Andersen's *The Snow Queen*. Allie plays the role of the ice girl who falls under the spell of the Snow Queen. The Snow Queen says that in seeking deeper snow for their games, children often become "lost souls" and end up in her world (160). She is a seductive enchantress, enticing children to forget about home and family and instead stay in her world, the world of frozen hearts. Allie's character in the play is strongly attracted to this idea. In yielding to the Snow Queen's control, she is transformed into the ice girl and is given the power to make things disappear, power that she ultimately uses on her little brother. Like the game called Death, this play reflects the adolescent fear of and simultaneous attraction to death. In playing this role—a role which she says she finds exhilarating—Allie, like Askew, is able to confront death and gain power over it. This role is an appropriate one for her in that it exemplifies the "self-absorbed" nature of Allie's creativity.[23]

The third story is the one Kit writes in response to a school assignment. It is the story of Lak, a prehistoric, Ice Age boy who sets out on a journey to rescue his baby sister when she is stolen by a marauding bear. When the children finally return to their family's cave, the family is gone, apparently having given up Lak and the baby for dead. Lak then treks southward, nurturing his sister along the way and finally reuniting with his family. This narrative is a coming-of-age story in which the adolescent main character goes out into the world and proves his worthiness to enter adulthood. But it is also a story of domesticity, nurturing, and a return to the hearth. Whereas Askew's solipsistic game represents the adolescent fear of and simultaneous attraction to the annihilation of self, and Allie's story represents a detached attitude toward family and community and a desire to control others through one's own selfish actions, Kit's story, in contrast, suggests a movement toward responsibility to others, the creation of self through connection to family and community.

The creative force of the novel lies in the tension among these various versions of self-creation. For each of the main characters, art provides a way of working out this tension and ultimately of negotiating the passage from childhood to young adulthood. For Allie, by far the most extroverted of the three main characters, self-creation means constantly playing a role. She is quite good, for example, at mimicking Kit's (now deceased) grandmother, winning accolades from Kit's amused grandfather (57). While playing the game called Death, she pretends to "die" and afterwards fabricates a story about having seen angels and devils, rivers and tunnels (40). She tells Kit proudly, "'Good bit of acting that'" (40). She is then astonished when Kit says that, when he "died," he was not pretending (56). Allie's acting gains the attention of the community, yet, ironically, it also distances her from them. She admits to Kit that her involvement with Askew and the other children stems not from a wish to be part of a social group, but instead from her desire to understand their actions so that she can imitate them: "'I'm going to be an actor,' she said. 'An artist. I need to see these things 'cause the day'll come when I'll be able to act the thickos out!'" (39). Allie seems most energized when she is performing. When she and Kit are threatened by Askew's father, she boldly stands up to him. But later she admits to Kit that her bravery was "'just an act'" (114). When she performs in the school play, she is so consumed by the role that the role begins to define her. Kit explains, "Allie was engulfed by *The Snow Queen*. She sparkled with the joy of it, so intensely that it seemed there truly was ice and frost in her eyes" (135). Allie finds acting exhilarating precisely because it allows her to create a variety of selves. One day as she and Kit are walking home from school, she wonders, somewhat whimsically, who she really is, and she admits it is the "magic" of role-playing that most appeals to her: "I don't just have to be me" (135).

While Allie is the extroverted performer, Askew is the introverted observer/recorder. His talent is drawing, and, along with the game called Death, it is his primary way of interacting with the world and thus defining himself. The first time Kit meets him, he notices that Askew is carrying a sketch pad and has a pencil tucked behind his ear (9). Askew then surprises Kit by giving him a drawing he made of Kit a few days earlier sitting by the fence at school staring down at the grass (11). Askew says proudly that he is the "[b]est artist in the school. Not that it counts for nothing in that blasted place" (11). This attitude, however, seems to be more a reflection of Askew's insecurities rather than reality. Several adults, including teachers and Kit's parents and grandfather, all acknowledge that Askew is a gifted artist, and, in fact, several of Askew's drawings are on display in the corridor at school (14). At the same time, adults mistrust him, perhaps partly because of his family background but also because he presents himself as a figure of darkness always lurking at the edges of the community. In a sense his art, much like Allie's acting, keeps him both visible in the community and at the same time marginalized, for he is the consummate artist/observer rather than an active participant. Like the adults, Kit recognizes the darkness in Askew and fears it, yet he also feels drawn to him and his art. Kit tells him that his drawing is "brilliant" (89) and that, in playing the role of the delinquent, he is wasting his talents. While Askew's art keeps him on the fringes of the community, it paradoxically serves as his way of engaging in social interactions with Kit. During the course of the novel, Askew creates several drawings, all connected to Kit in some way: Silky, the little ghost boy of the pit, inspired by Kit's version of his grandfather's story; Askew and Kit in the cave, nearly naked and facing each other with knives; a Christmas card for Kit, depicting the wilderness with a Christmas tree in it surrounded by children; and the illustrations for Kit's story of Lak. For Askew, the process of artistic creation serves as his way of defining himself and of forging a deeper connection to Kit.

Kit is drawn to both Allie's overt theatricality and Askew's brooding introversion, but he is much less self-absorbed than either of them. He defines himself through his work as a writer and storyteller, and he has garnered a measure of recognition through his stories. Askew, for example, mentions having seen one of Kit's stories displayed on the wall at school. This is the story of the ghost boy Silky, a story that Kit's grandfather told him, which Kit refashioned into his own story and which Askew describes as "brilliant" (15). Kit's teacher, the one the children call "Burning Bush," appreciates Kit's talent too, but she also recognizes the power and danger of his imagination. After the children have been caught playing the game called Death, Burning Bush admonishes Kit: "No need to act the stories out. . . . The words are enough" (78). Later, Mr. Chambers, the school administrator, warns

Kit that "the darkness" should be kept in books or on the stage (163). Kit's imagination, like Askew's, is powerful, but it also has a dark edge to it.

As a storyteller, Kit is not just a writer, but also a performer, somewhat like Allie. Burning Bush, in giving a writing assignment, describes how ancient storytellers held their listeners enthralled (99–100). Allie, with her acutely developed theatrical sense, equates the ancient storytellers with magicians, people who were given special caves because they were both revered and feared by the community (128). Kit develops as a storyteller with this kind of power in his community. It is not unusual when he is crossing the wilderness for the younger children to call out to him, begging him for a story (101). A number of scholars have discussed the importance and power of stories in human development.[24] And Almond himself said, in his Michael L. Printz Award acceptance speech, that *Kit's Wilderness* is "a book that depends on storytelling, on the passing-down of information and inspiration from generation to generation."[25] Certainly, Kit's creative powers as a storyteller facilitate his psychic well-being. When his ill grandfather wanders out into the snow and collapses, Kit finds that his story of Lak keeps running through his head in spite of the fact that he tries to focus on his grandfather's plight (121). Although Kit may not be consciously aware of it, it seems clear that his psyche has summoned this fictional story to help him deal with a real-life traumatic experience. Later, at the hospital, Kit tells his catatonic grandfather his own version of the story of Silky as a way of helping his grandfather regain his grip on reality (145–47). The story has now come full circle. Kit first heard this story from his grandfather, transformed it into his own, and now is able to use it to conjure an almost magical power to help his grandfather emerge from the darkness of his coma. Similarly, in the climactic scene of the novel, Kit tells the story of Lak to Askew as the two boys huddle together in the cave. As a result, Askew's destructive desires are abated and replaced with a bond of friendship between Askew and Kit. The story further helps facilitate Askew's resocialization, for he eventually agrees to return to Stoneygate and his family.

Kit's story illustrates the transformative power of both the imagination and narrative, and its prominence in the novel suggests its importance in Kit's developing identity. This story within a story constitutes a significant part of the novel, appearing in chapters 10, 12, 14, 22, and 32. The power of the story is evident in the effect it has on Kit as he composes it. It invades his dreams, for instance, to the extent that his identity becomes intertwined with Lak's (131). However, rather than feeling that his identity is being erased, Kit feels empowered by the process of writing and telling the story. When Allie says that acting is invigorating because it allows one to change the world (135), Kit realizes this is a lesson about the creative process he has already learned from his stories and dreams (135).

Kit's story of Lak, although written in response to a school assignment, is inspired by Askew, just as Askew's drawings are inspired by Kit. Moreover, the character of Lak embodies traits of both Kit and Askew. That the story is inspired by Askew is clearly indicated when Kit tells Allie that he's writing the story not just for their teacher, but for John Askew as well (153). Later, in the cave, Kit tells Askew the same thing (188). In some ways, the story of Lak is not just a story Kit has written *for* Askew—it is also a story *about* Askew. Both Askew and Lak suffer abuse at the hands of their fathers, and both must define themselves in opposition to their fathers. In composing the story, Kit merges Askew's life with Lak's story in such a way that he becomes convinced of their interconnectedness: "'I think if Lak and his sister're safe, then Askew'll be safe. And if he's safe, they'll be safe'" (154). Kit also makes a connection between Askew and Lak when his grandfather says that Askew "'never had a proper childhood, not with that for a father. The baby inside him never had a chance to grow'" (110). Kit wonders, "Where *was* the baby in him? And I thought of Lak, whose baby was so obvious, held inside the bearskin" (110). While hearing the story, Askew too senses the connection between himself and Lak. He later tells Kit that he dreamed of the baby "'[l]ike the boy in the story'" (203). He continues, "'There was a space against my heart where she once was and I needed her there to fill it again'" (203). As Brennan has noted, several of Almond's novels involve adolescent characters experiencing a transformative encounter with their inner child.[26] Through Kit's story, Askew is able to reconnect with the child inside of himself and to connect with Kit as well.

All along Askew has told Kit that they are alike, although this is an idea that Kit has resisted even while recognizing that he is inexplicably attracted to Askew. Throughout the novel, the relationship between Kit and Askew is characterized by what Eve Kosofsky Sedgwick calls "male homosocial desire," i.e., the rather amorphous continuum (or "wilderness" perhaps?) between male bonding and homoerotic desire, a continuum that is disrupted and thus rendered largely invisible in male society.[27] Initially, Kit is afraid of Askew and yet feels strangely attracted to him. When Askew tells him early in their relationship that Kit's stories are much like his own drawings, Kit admits, "My hands trembled and my flesh crawled, but I felt myself being drawn to him" (15). Brennan offers a compelling insight into the complex relationship between Kit and Askew: "John both resents and needs Kit, who can lead him towards reconciliation with his family; Kit both fears and needs John and his commitment to their shared history."[28] In the climactic scene in the abandoned mine, Kit finally acknowledges their interconnection: "'We're joined in blood'" (203). It is ironic that Allie sees herself as the boys' rescuer, for, in fact, it is the boys' own ability, facilitated by Kit's story, to establish a bond between themselves that saves them. Kit's story transforms both boys, and helps them forge their identities as well as their friendship. It is fitting, then, that Askew illustrates the story of Lak, with great success. Their teacher says that the words and pictures "'are like the heart and soul of the same story'" (228).

Rorty reminds us that self-creation can never be completed "because there is nothing to complete, there is only a web of relations to be rewoven, a web which time lengthens every day."[29] We should, then, "be content to think of any human life as the always incomplete, yet sometimes heroic, reweaving of such a web."[30] Almond's achievement in *Kit's Wilderness* lies in his ability to skillfully interconnect the theme of self-creation with the themes of artistic creation, family and community, and the reality of death. Kit, through his ability to transform stories from the past, create "new" stories, and share these stories in written and oral performances, exemplifies Almond's notion that "[w]e're interwoven with those who have gone, with those who are here now, with those who are to come."[31] He achieves a measure of heroism in creating an identity through art as he negotiates the difficult passage from childhood to adulthood.

Notes

1. Roberta Seelinger Trites, *Disturbing the Universe: Power and Repression in Adolescent Literature* (Iowa City, IA: University of Iowa Press, 2000) 117.

2. Erica Wagner, "Could a Children's Book Win the Booker?" rev. of *Kit's Wilderness*, by David Almond, *The Times* [London] 20 May 1999, *Lexis-Nexis*, online, 4 June 2003.

3. Elizabeth Bush, rev. of *Kit's Wilderness*, by David Almond, *Bulletin of the Center for Children's Books* 53.5 (2000), *Children's Literature Reviews, Children's Literature Comprehensive Database*, online, 29 May 2003.

4. Susan P. Bloom, rev. of *Kit's Wilderness*, by David Almond, *Horn Book* 76.2 (2000): 192.

5. Ilene Cooper, rev. of *Kit's Wilderness*, by David Almond, *Booklist* 96.9 and 10 (2000), *Children's Literature Reviews, Children's Literature Comprehensive Database*, online, 29 May 2003.

6. Rev. of *Kit's Wilderness*, by David Almond, *Cooperative Children's Book Center Choice* 2001, *Children's Literature Reviews, Children's Literature Comprehensive Database*, online, 29 May 2003.

7. Kathleen Odean, rev. of *Kit's Wilderness*, by David Almond, *Book* (May 2001): 80.

8. Ellen Fader, rev. of *Kit's Wilderness*, by David Almond, *School Library Journal* 46.3 (2000): 233.

9. Enicia Fisher, rev. of *Kit's Wilderness*, by David Almond, *Christian Science Monitor* 92.94 (2000): 15.

10. Bette Ammon, rev. of *Kit's Wilderness*, by David Almond, *VOYA* 23.1 (2000), *Children's Literature Reviews, Children's Literature Comprehensive Database*, online, 29 May 2003.

11. Ken Donelson, rev. of *Kit's Wilderness*, by David Almond, *English Journal* 91.2 (2001): 116–17.

12. Richard Rorty, *Contingency, Irony, and Solidarity* (New York: Cambridge University Press, 1989) 37.

13. Rorty, *Contingency, Irony, and Solidarity*, 24.

14. Rorty, *Contingency, Irony, and Solidarity*, 27.

15. Rorty, *Contingency, Irony, and Solidarity*, 33.

16. Rorty, *Contingency, Irony, and Solidarity*, 43.

17. Wendy B. Faris, *Ordinary Enchantments: Magical Realism and the Remystification of Narrative* (Nashville, TN: Vanderbilt University Press, 2004) 25–26.

18. Nina Auberbach, *Private Theatricals: The Lives of the Victorians* (Cambridge, MA: Harvard University Press, 1990) 36.

19. David Almond, "The 2001 Michael L. Printz Award Acceptance Speech," *Journal of Youth Services in Libraries* 14.4 (2001): 15, *WilsonSelectPlus*, online, 13 February 2003.

20. David Almond, "Afterword," *Wild Girl Wild Boy: A Play* (London: Hodder Children's Books, 2002) 86–87.

21. Trites, *Disturbing the Universe*, 118–19.

22. Geraldine Brennan, "The Game Called Death: Frightening Fictions by David Almond, Philip Gross, and Lesley Howarth," *Frightening Fiction: R. L. Stine, Robert Westall, David Almond, and Others*, ed. Kimberly Reynolds, Geraldine Brennan, and Kevin McCarron (New York: Continuum, 2001) 103.

23. Brennanm, "The Game Called Death," 104.

24. See, for example, Bruno Bettelheim, *The Uses of Enchantment: The Meaning and Importance of Fairy Tales* (New York: Knopf, 1976; Vintage–Random, 1989), and Robert Coles, *The Call of Stories: Teaching and the Moral Imagination* (Boston: Houghton Mifflin, 1989).

25. Almond, "The 2001 Michael L. Printz Award Acceptance Speech," 23.

26. Brennan, "The Game Called Death," 99.

27. Eve Kosofsky Sedgwick, *Between Men: English Literature and Male Homosocial Desire* (New York: Columbia University Press, 1985) 1–2.

28. Brennan, "The Game Called Death," 106.

29. Rorty, *Contingency, Irony, and Solidarity*, 42–43.

30. Rorty, *Contingency, Irony, and Solidarity*, 43.

31. Almond, "The 2001 Michael L. Printz Award Acceptance Speech," 23.

CHAPTER FIVE

Damaged Children: *Heaven Eyes*

Published in the United Kingdom in 2000 and the United States in 2001, *Heaven Eyes* was in many ways Almond's darkest novel up to that point. In retrospect, it has proven to be part of a trend toward depictions of increasingly darker situations and more overt criticism of social ills. The novel tells the story of three orphans who take a journey downriver to escape, at least momentarily, life at Whitegates, a home for what their caretaker describes as "damaged" children who have lost their parents. Their intended destination is the sea, but they end up at the Black Middens, a muddy, blighted landscape filled with dilipated warehouses along the banks of the Tyne River. Amid this desolate wasteland they meet the strange child known as "Heaven Eyes" and the demented old man she calls "Grampa." Ironically, they do not travel very far from Whitegates, at least not in geographic terms. Psychologically, however, they are transformed in profound ways, so that, when they return to Whitegates, they do so with a stronger sense of their own identities. Like Almond's earlier novels, *Heaven Eyes* emphasizes the importance of memories and stories while employing elements of magical realism to effect the psychic transformation of its adolescent characters.

Following the tremendous success of *Skellig* and *Kit's Wilderness*, *Heaven Eyes* was eagerly awaited and reviewed widely. Reviewers praised Almond for his "lyrical and dreamlike" writing,[1] and for his skillful and moving combination of realism and mysticism. Ilene Cooper found the novel intriguing, both "gritty" and "pure," although nearly impossible to classify. Is it allegory or fantasy? she wondered: "Certainly Almond is one of the foremost practitioners in children's literature of magical realism. Yet when it comes to the emotions the story contains, no book could be more true."[2] *The Horn Book Guide* reviewer admired Almond's achievement in creating "an elusive tale, shrouded in mysteries, laced with the supernatural, and filled with often startling imagery."[3] Lyn Gardner described the story as "a beautiful, eerie tale" about "daring to go as far as death and having the bravery to come back again."[4] *Kirkus Reviews* praised the vividly realized surreal setting and the rich symbolism, but felt that some readers might find the ending, where the mother of one of the orphans suddenly returns, to be a bit too tidy. Still, the reviewer added, "Almond is essentially an idealist and readers will be satisfied."[5] Interestingly, Florence H. Munat admired the novel because the "ending is not tidy" and it holds appeal for both younger and older readers.[6] Although the book received no major literary awards, it was named to numerous "best book" lists, including *Booklist* Books for Youth Editor's Choice, *Publishers Weekly* Best Books, the American Library Association's Notable Books for Children, and Bank Street College of Education's Best Children's Books of the Year. With *Heaven Eyes*, Almond established himself as one of the major voices in children's and young adult literature for the new millennium.

The narrator of the novel is Erin Law, an adolescent girl who has come to live at Whitegates in the city of St. Gabriel's after her mother's death. Her friends and fellow travelers are the bitterly defiant January Carr and the "gentle and timid" (8) Sean "Mouse" Gullane. Another child living at Whitegates is the nearly autistic but very creative Wilson Cairns. The caretaker of these "damaged children," as she calls them, is Maureen, a woman whose profound sadness and despair suggest that she may be even more damaged than her charges. January builds a raft from old door panels and talks Erin into running away downriver with him. When Mouse sees them about to leave, he begs them to let him go along. They do not get very far, however, before their raft founders in the mud of the Black Middens.

They are rescued by Heaven Eyes, a mysterious girl with large eyes and webbed fingers and toes who lives in an abandoned printing works with a senile old man she calls "Grampa." During their surreal experience on the Black Middens, the children discover a "saint" buried in the mud, find a box of newspaper clippings about Heaven Eyes' real family's demise at sea, and witness Grampa's death. The children return to Whitegates, taking Heaven Eyes with them. January goes to live with his mother, who has suddenly reappeared. Heaven Eyes assumes her real name, Anna May, but retains her almost magical sensibility and helps to transform Maureen's despair into hope. And Erin, largely because of her experiences on the Black Middens, is finally able to tell her life story and thus begin her own transformation into adulthood.

Recovering the Past

Heaven Eyes echoes many of the themes in Almond's previous novels. We have already seen, for example, portraits of "damaged" people, namely in the characters of Loosa Fine and Jack Law in *Counting Stars*, and John Askew and his father in *Kit's Wilderness*. The term "damaged children" is an imposed label that Erin rejects, but in many ways these children have been damaged by the circumstances of their lives, though not irrevocably, as Maureen thinks. Almond's ongoing concern with the effects of death and loss is certainly present in *Heaven Eyes*, for all of the children have lost their parents through either death or abandonment. The importance of memory, of developing and/or preserving connections to the past, is another theme emphasized in *Heaven Eyes*. For the children of Whitegates their memories, and perhaps a few artifacts and faded photographs, are all they have to remind them of their parents and to build their identities. Self-creation is intimately bound with memories of family, as Maureen seems to understand. She tells the children that it is important for them to be able to tell their life stories even if they are "a mixture of fact and memory and imagination" (6).

And, like Almond's other works, *Heaven Eyes* is especially concerned with the spiritual dimension of life, with the magic just behind the surface of reality and with the special ability of young people to recognize that magic. The child Heaven Eyes, with her mysterious, other worldly qualities, reminds us of Skellig in many ways. Similarly, the ability of the children to see the ghosts of Grampa and the saint remind us of Kit's and Askew's ability to see the ghost children from the mine pit. And Erin's internalization of her mother's spirit is, as we will see, much like Joe Maloney's internalization of the tiger's spirit in *Secret Heart*. The children's highly developed spiritual capacity proves to be crucial in helping them to develop their adult identities, in helping them to believe, as Erin says, that "[w]e can do anything we want to do" (18).

In other ways, though, *Heaven Eyes* represents a significant departure for Almond. For one thing, this is his only novel with a female narrator. While all of his novels feature strong, multifaceted female characters—and Erin Law certainly fits that description—she is the only female (to date) given the role of narrator. Another significant difference between this novel and Almond's other works is that in this novel the adults, at least the ones who are living, seem seriously flawed in some way. Maureen, although deeply concerned with her charges' welfare, is too damaged herself to see the true beauty and potential of the children she cares for. Similarly, Grampa, while fiercely affectionate toward and protective of Heaven Eyes, is also senile to the point of dementia. The orphaned girl takes care of him as much as he takes care of her. Both Maureen and Grampa look to the children to validate their own existence and in that sense they exploit, albeit without malice, those they love. The exception to this is Erin's mother, whose spirit is palpably present in her daughter's life. Erin thinks of the time before her mother's death as a kind of paradise, and she continues to draw strength and guidance from her vivid memories of her mother. Moreover, she encourages Heaven Eyes to draw similar strength from her memories of her own mother. The only truly effective adult role models in the novel are deceased; it is through their children's memories that they exert a transformative influence.

A Mythic Journey

Heaven Eyes, like all of Almond's novels, involves a journey of self-discovery and self-creation. The structure of the narrative is circular, with the book being divided into three parts, each corresponding to a geographical location: it starts out in Whitegates, moves to the Black Middens, and then returns to Whitegates. We learn at the outset what will happen, for Erin tells us about her and her friends' journey, their encounter with Heaven Eyes and Grampa, and the "saint" they discover in the black mud. We learn that these children have taken such journeys before. But this is the first time the children have used the river as a means of escape. To them, the river represents the thrill of adventure, the seductive potential for danger, and ultimately the hope of freedom.

Ironically, their trip downriver turns out to be only a short distance, yet it has profound psychological significance for the children. Florence H. Munat describes this trip as "a metaphor for life's journey,"[7] while Janice M. Del Negro notes that it "closely hew[s] to the traditions of the hero's journey (the children set forth, enter a different world, encounter mystery and danger, exhibit bravery and save the princess) . . . "[8] In that sense, the structure and plot echo a number of classic texts of both adult and children's literature. Almond has acknowledged that the opening sentence—"My name is Erin Law" (3) is an homage to the famous opening of Herman Melville's *Moby Dick*: "Call me Ishmael."[9] Also, the motif of a river raft journey that leads to greater self-awareness recalls Mark Twain's *Huckleberry Finn*. Such intertextual allusions highlight the mythic dimensions of the children's journey as well as the magical and transformative aspects of their experience.

The various settings reinforce the mythic nature of the children's journey. Whitegates is the societal institution, providing for physical needs but offering little in the way of spiritual sustenance. It is a three-story building with a garden paved over in concrete and enclosed by a metal fence. Although Erin points out that the place is not intended to be a prison, its appearance certainly suggests that function. The river is the children's route to freedom, the means by which they travel from Whitegates to the Black Middens and back again. More broadly, it represents the passage of time, both constant and constantly changing, connecting the past to the present and the present to the future. The river also represents danger, and for the children, this is part of its attraction. Like the children of *Kit's Wilderness* who play the game called Death, Erin and her friends are thrilled by the opportunity to confront death.

The Black Middens, a place of wet, black mud, is a middle ground, a kind of liminal territory between the solidity of the land and the fluidity of the river. It represents a kind of primordial chaos, a place where "treasures" can be found, and the place from which Heaven Eyes and, later, Erin and her friends are rescued. It is also the place where Mouse finds the "saint," a dead sailor from long ago whose corpse has been preserved by the mud and the silt. Like the wilderness in *Kit's Wilderness* and *Wild Girl, Wild Boy*, the Black Middens may also be seen as a metaphor for the creative imagination. Close beside are the abandoned warehouses and printing works where Heaven Eyes and Grampa live. Once a thriving industrial district, the area has now fallen into neglect and decay, a victim of changing economic times. At least one reviewer has noted the parallel between the unknown pasts of many of the orphans and the soon-to-be-forgotten history of these warehouses.[10] But, just as a dilapidated garage gives shelter to an angel in *Skellig*, the Black Middens proves to be a place with magical beings, for it is here that the orphans meet Heaven Eyes, Grampa, and the saint. It is also a place of rebirth. Literally, the place itself is being revitalized. Even as the children are leaving to return to Whitegates, cranes and wrecking balls are moving in to clear out the old buildings in order to make way for new development. The saint too is reborn, rising from the dead to escort Grampa's soul to the river. And the children themselves are reborn here in the sense that their experience changes them in profound ways and helps in the formation of their adult identities. They enter the Black Middens as damaged children, but they emerge as adults, restored and ready to actively create their life stories.

Damaged People

Most of the characters in the novel, both children and adults, are "damaged" in various ways. However, they also possess the potential to be psychologically restored and spiritually renewed. Maureen often tells the children that with her help they can become "the finest of folk" (5), but in reality she has a hard time believing this herself. In spite of her best intentions, she sees the children as "damaged, and beyond repair" (5). To be sure, these children have had difficult lives. In many ways, they are psychologically and/or physically damaged. Erin lost her mother through death, January was left as an infant at the door to a hospital, and Mouse was abandoned by his father with the words "please look after me" tattooed on his arm. Other children, the victims of abuse or neglect, have presumably been taken away from their parents by the state. Although Erin rejects the label "damaged," even she admits that many of the children at Whitegates are sad and bitter, with "broken hearts and troubled souls" (5). At the same time, most of them have been able to create a family among themselves by loving and caring for one another, and in so doing they have been able to "find a tiny corner of the Paradise that [they'd] all lost" (6). This is the only way they have been able to survive the parade of well-intentioned but clearly ineffectual societal representatives, such as psychologists, social workers, and play therapists. The implication is clear: by connecting with one another, the children have survived in spite of, not because of, society's interventions.

The child characters respond in different ways to the damage they have suffered, but clearly identity is an issue for each of them. Erin holds onto the few artifacts her mother left behind—a couple of photographs, a lock of hair, lipstick, nail polish, and perfume. These items constitute the palpable part of her memories of "Paradise" (22) that she and her mother shared in the small house where they lived. Now she resists forming a meaningful relationship with another adult, as is evident in her refusal to cooperate with Maureen and write her own Life Story book. Erin admits that she sometimes experiences "pain and darkness" so deep that she is afraid she will "not get out again" (9). January knows nothing of his mother, having been abandoned when he was an infant. However, he firmly believes that his mother will one day return to claim him. In the meantime, he too resists Maureen's attempts to help him, and he refuses to write his Life Story book. Instead, he takes pleasure in concocting new schemes for escaping from Whitegates. His pain and bitterness are evident in his preference for dressing in black (much like John Askew), his mockery of Heaven Eyes, and his distrust of Grampa. Mouse, who was abandoned by his father, is an especially sensitive child who gives in readily to Maureen's cajoling. He takes refuge in digging for "treasure," recovering broken toys and other such items that, like him, have been cast off as no longer useful. Wilson Cairns, whose past has included neglect and abuse, sits and stares at the wall, rarely speaking. He finds solace in fashioning small people out of lumps of clay. According to Maureen, this is his way to "re-create some of the childhood he had lost" (29). More likely, this is his way to *create* a childhood he never had. Wilson is yet another of Almond's child characters who is able to find meaning for his life and forge his identity through artistic expression.

The concern with identity in *Heaven Eyes* can be seen clearly in the focus on the names of the children. As Geraldine Brennan has noted, "Names are important to these children: names are all they have."[11] Moreover, their names indicate their origins and in that sense lend them an identity. Erin Law has the name given to her by her mother, but January's name was created by the circumstances under which he was abandoned. He was left on the steps of Carr Hospital in the bitter month of January. The name seems appropriate, for his identity is shaped, still, by the circumstance of his adandonment. He can be cold to people he does not trust, which for him is most people, and his bitterness is always lurking just beneath the surface. Mouse's real name is Sean, but he is called Mouse because of the small pet mouse he carries in his pocket. The name fits him because he too is small, sensitive, and fragile. Similar to a mouse, he likes to forage, and he is skittish, easily upset by the words of others. Later, Grampa gives him the name of "Little Helper" when he begins assisting the old man in digging for treasure. Heaven Eyes also has a name that is not her birth name. When Grampa finds her in the mud of the Black Middens, he christens her "Heaven Eyes," because of her ability "to see through all the darkness in the world to the joy that lies beneath" (4). Her real name, we later discover, is Anna May, an equally beautiful name that suggests the month of spring and joy. The name "May" contrasts with the name "January" just as the dispositions of the two children stand in sharp contrast. Whereas January is bitter and distrustful, often focusing only on the darkness, Anna May is trusting and loving, always seeing the good in everything. It is not surprising then that, while January initially mocks Anna, she eventually helps him to see through the darkness to the restorative power of the magic that is in the world.

The multiplicity of names also suggests the fluidity of identity. When January's mother returns, she reclaims her son and gives him the new name "Gabriel Jones." Similarly, after Grampa dies and Heaven

Eyes comes to live at Whitegates, she reverts to her birth name "Anna May." In both cases, the "new" names symbolize new circumstances and new identities, but they also represent a return to the past, to each child's origins. The connection between names and the fluidity of identity can be seen both literally and metaphorically when Mouse picks up metal type from the floor of the abandoned printing works and spells each child's name. Limited by what letters he can find and, perhaps, by the fact that he is not a very good speller, Mouse produces names that are a mixture of typefaces, type sizes, and uppercase and lowercase letters. The result is an amalgam of letters, suggesting each child's identity and uniqueness. These "damaged" names suggest the damage these children have suffered, and the children's reactions to their names indicate their insistence on defining themselves. To Heaven Eyes, who has never learned to read, the letters are gibberish, yet she is intrigued by Mouse's statement that "'[t]he letters make words and the words make us'" (66). She looks at the letters that spell (actually misspell) her own name and pronounces them to be "'lovely'" (p. 66). January, on the other hand, kicks the letters of his name away, complaining that they look like letters on a tombstone.

Most of the adults in the novel are damaged in some way as well—and, it could be argued, in more profound ways than the children. Maureen, for example, is often heard weeping at night behind her closed door. She wanders the corridors at night, unable to sleep, and her eyes betray a "strange mixture of love and bitterness" (5). Rumor has it that Maureen could have no children, or that she lost a child, but no one really knows the source of her pain. Grampa, too, is damaged, although his affliction seems more mental than psychological, most likely the effects of old age. He has trouble remembering even the simplest things, so he writes everything down in his big ledger. He is also suffering from paranoia. The word "Security" on his tattered uniform serves as an ironic comment on the extreme insecurity he feels in trying to protect his small world from the intrusion of outsiders. At the same time, the label emphasizes his role in Heaven Eyes' life, for he does provide her with a sense of security. The door to his office reads "C RET KER" (59), alluding perhaps to his former, and now defunct, occupation. With his almost comic uniform (it has epaulettes), the deteriorating sign on his office door, and the big black ledger into which he scribbles the minutiae of each day, Grampa seems like a parody of a ruined god, no longer capable of performing his role as deity. And yet he does perform the role of caretaker, however erratically, for Heaven Eyes—at least until her true story is discovered by January. After Grampa dies, the "saint" rises from the dead to escort his soul to the river, an act that ultimately attests to the dignity of the old man's life and death.

Death and Rebirth

The rich imagery of the novel reinforces the themes of death and rebirth as they relate to the children's evolving identities. The raft that the children use for their escape, for example, is one January has fashioned out of three doors marked "Enter," "Danger," and "Exit." Literally, the doors facilitate an (albeit temporary) exit from Whitegates and an entrance into the world of the Black Middens, Grampa, and Heaven Eyes. Metaphorically, they represent the transition from one psychological realm to another. The journey itself holds both risk and promise, and, in fact, the children nearly are swallowed up by the mud of the Black Middens. The dilapidated warehouses reflect "the ruins of the past" (9), and, in their abandoned and damaged state, they also parallel the lives of the orphans who take shelter there. At the same time, they retain traces of their former glory. The scattered type on the floor of the old printing works is suggestive of the stories that once came out of this place, while the statues of angels and eagles on the old machines lend the warehouse the aura of a ruined church. At the same time, these images represent the persistence of the magical among the mundane and, as such, serve as an apt metaphor for the magical potential within the "damaged" children who have been washed ashore there.

Another key image and recurring motif are the various photographs that represent the children's connection to their pasts and, as such, are invested with an almost fetishistic quality because, in one way or another, they help the children to define their identities. Erin has a photograph of herself and her mother in the garden of their house in St. Gabriel's, and she also has an ultrasound photograph of herself as an embryo growing inside her mother's womb. Along with other artifacts that her mother left behind, these photographs provide Erin with both solace and a sense of identity. She cherishes these photographs because they represent a connection to her mother. Mouse also has a photograph that he cherishes, allegedly a picture of his father. In it, a group of men can be seen playing soccer, although the images are so small that it is hard to see what anyone really looks like. Mouse is not even certain which man is his real father, but he holds on to this photograph because it is all he has. In contrast to the strong presence of Erin's mother—both in Erin's photographs and in her life—Mouse's father is nothing more than an illusive trace on a piece of celluloid. And January's discovery of the faded pictures of Heaven Eyes and her family, which Grampa has kept hidden away along with newspaper accounts of the family's disappearance at sea, allow the child to look into, and thus begin to recover, her past.

For the children, identity formation is closely intertwined with recovering the past and discovering the presence of the mystical in the everyday world. One mystical connection for Erin is her dead mother's presence, a presence so strong that it is almost palpable. Erin often feels her mother's touch and smells her mother's perfume. Her memories of her mother keep her from giving up hope and, as she says, from going so far into the darkness that she can never come out again. Her mother is the force that rescues her when she is about to sink into the mud of the Black Middens. More than just a vivid memory, Erin's mother serves as her guardian angel. Yet, while Erin's mother is a source of strength as well as a connection to Erin's childhood, somehow that is not quite enough to allow Erin to form her own adult identity. It is the mysterious child Heaven Eyes who helps Erin to see the joy behind all of the pain and darkness in the world and ultimately to tell her own story. Heaven Eyes initially thinks that Erin is her sister, and this is a role Erin willingly accepts. Earlier, Erin has said that, before her mother died, she often fantasized about her mother remarrying and having more children: "And in my dreams I saw them, those brothers and sisters" (24). While the other children of Whitegates have served as her surrogate family, Erin responds to Heaven Eyes as if she is the sister she dreamed about but never had. This elfin child, with her webbed fingers and webbed toes and her "moon-round, watery blue" eyes (53), brings out the maternal side of Erin. She provides Erin with an opportunity both to stop focusing on her lost childhood and, at the same time, to recover it vicariously. In many ways, Heaven Eyes is the embodiment of the quintessential Romantic child: innocent, joyous, and yet strangely wise beyond her years. Erin, who seems stuck in an idealized view of the past, is transformed by this child who seemingly has no past.

While both Heaven Eyes and the spirit of Erin's mother represent mystical elements in the novel, they are, strictly speaking, not quite magical. Rational explanations can be posited for each. Heaven Eyes, as it turns out, is not from another world but is instead an orphan whose family was lost at sea. Her peculiar speech patterns, which lend her an otherworldly quality, are actually something she has picked up from Grampa. Likewise, we do not have to interpret Erin's mother as a ghost. Instead, her strong presence in the novel can be attributed to her daughter's vivid imagination and powerful memories.

However, there are other magical elements in the novel that cannot be explained rationally. One is the apparent animation of Wilson Cairns's clay figures, and the other is the resurrection of the saint to escort Grampa's soul to the river. In both cases, more than one child witnesses the event and in effect provides confirmation of the magic. Furthermore, the magical nature of these two incidents calls into question any rational explanations we may posit for the other seemingly magical events. This is the typical effect of magical realism: to subvert rational explanations for extraordinary phenomena. The end result is that, while we need not resort to supernatural explanations to explain the presence of Erin's mother, for example, we may not easily dismiss such explanations either. In other words, Erin's mother may be a ghost, and that is how at least one reviewer interprets her, noting that when Erin "feels her mother's arms around her, hears her voice in her ear," these things occur "not in memory, but in reality."[12]

The most obviously magical event of the novel is the resurrection of the saint, which parallels the children's spiritual resurrection. Like the children, the saint is dug out of the Black Middens, and like the children, he experiences a miraculous rebirth. His purpose in coming back to life is to escort Grampa's soul to the river, where they disappear beneath the water, symbolically joining the continuous flow of past, present, and future. Soon thereafter, the children too return to the river, either to resume their journey or to return to Whitegates. Their decision to return to Whitegates takes them back to a life they have known, but they are not the same children they were before. Having witnessed the "saint's" resurrection, they are prepared to experience their own rebirth. No longer children, not quite adults, they now have the capacity to tell their own stories and to forge their own identities.

The power of stories, and more specifically of storytelling, is emphasized throughout the novel. At Whitegates, Erin has resisted telling her story, for she sees the Life Story book as a meaningless tool devised by ineffectual adults. And perhaps she is right; perhaps she knows intuitively that her story cannot be produced on demand, but must be nurtured and given birth at the appropriate time. For Erin, that time comes after she meets Heaven Eyes and takes the younger child into her care. Then she is able to tell her own story, along with the story of her companions, stories that flow into one another "like the twisting currents of a river" (232). She is also able, along with January, to tell Heaven Eyes her life story that they have pieced together from the newspaper accounts discovered in Grampa's office and the ramblings they have deciphered from his black book. They tell the story gradually, while Erin, like a mother cradling her child, holds Heaven Eyes and comforts her as "the secrets" of her past enter into her consciousness (218).

Like all of Almond's works, *Heaven Eyes* focuses on the issue of adolescent identity development and its connection to memory and the creative imagination. This is shown to be an ongoing process filled with "great joy and magic" (232). As Erin says, the stories of the children of Whitegates could have been "sad sad tales" (232), but they are not. And the fact that they are not has much to do with the children's connections to one another. In the end, such connections—to one another, to the past, and to their own stories—allow these children to create identities for themselves in spite of society's having failed them. Erin, who has all along resisted telling her life story, ultimately embraces the idea of life as a story, affirming that "astounding things can lie waiting as each day dawns, as each page turns" (232).

Notes

1. See Paula Rohrlick, rev. of *Heaven Eyes*, by David Almond, *KLIATT Review* 35.2 (2001), *Children's Literature Reviews*, *Children's Literature Comprehensive*

Database, online, 29 May 2003; and Florence H. Munat, rev. of *Heaven Eyes*, by David Almond, *VOYA* 24.1 (2001), *Children's Literature Reviews*, *Children's Literature Comprehensive Database*, online, 29 May 2003.

2. Ilene Cooper, rev. of *Heaven Eyes*, by David Almond, *Booklist* 97.9 (2001), *Children's Literature Reviews*, *Children's Literature Comprehensive Database*, online, 29 May 2003.

3. Rev. of *Heaven Eyes*, by David Almond, *Horn Book Guide* 12.2 (2001), *Children's Literature Reviews*, *Children's Literature Comprehensive Database*, online, 29 May 2003.

4. Lyn Gardner, rev. of *Heaven Eyes*, by David Almond, *Education Guardian.co.uk*, 29 March 2000, *Guardian Unlimited*, online, 1 September 2005, http://education.guardian.co.uk/childrensbooks/11plus/review/0,,153450,00.htm.

5. Rev. of *Heaven Eyes*, by David Almond, *Kirkus Reviews* 69.4 (2001), *Children's Literature Reviews*, *Children's Literature Comprehensive Database*, online, 29 May 2003.

6. Munat, rev. of *Heaven Eyes*.

7. Munat, rev. of *Heaven Eyes*.

8. Janice M. Del Negro, rev. of *Heaven Eyes*, by David Almond, *Bulletin of the Center for Children's Books* 54.8 (2001), *Children's Literature Reviews*, *Children's Literature Comprehensive Database*, online, 29 May 2003.

9. David Almond, online chat session, *Blast*, BBC [n.d.], online, 9 March 2005, www.bbc.co.uk/blast/about/ask/dalmond_transcript.shtml.

10. Sharon Salluzzo, rev. of *Heaven Eyes*, by David Almond, *Children's Literature* 2001, *Children's Literature Reviews*, *Children's Literature Comprehensive Database*, online, 29 May 2003.

11. Geraldine Brennan, "The Game Called Death: Frightening Fictions by David Almond, Philip Gross, and Lesley Howarth," *Frightening Fiction: R. L. Stine, Robert Westall, David Almond, and Others*, eds. Kimberly Reynolds, Geraldine Brennan, and Kevin McCarron (New York: Continuum, 2001) 107.

12. Sarah Johnson, "Touching Tale of an Escape, a Journey and a Magical Child," rev. of *Heaven Eyes*, by David Almond, *The Times* [London] 20 January 2000, *Lexis-Nexis*, online, 4 June 2003.

CHAPTER SIX

The Forests of the Night: *Wild Girl, Wild Boy*; *Secret Heart*; and *Kate, the Cat and the Moon*

The close connection between children and the natural world is a theme with which Almond is clearly fascinated. We need only recall the image of David and his siblings imitating the circus animals in "Buffalo Camel Llama Zebra Ass" (*Counting Stars*), or the metaphorical associations between the children and the birds in *Skellig*. Moreover, it is a theme he has continued to explore in several subsequent works, including a play, a novel, and, more recently, a picture book. It is to those three works that we now turn our attention.

Wild Girl, Wild Boy

As Almond tells it, the genesis of *Wild Girl, Wild Boy* was in a request from Sally Goldsworthy, head of education at the Lyric Theatre, Hammersmith, London, to write a play for children. While contemplating the idea, he recalled the time he spent as a child in his grandfather's allotment pruning flowers and harvesting vegetables. He recalled the smell of the soil, the sounds of children playing in the distance, and the singing of larks high in the sky above.[1] That memory was folded into the play, along with painful memories of his own father's death. The result was *Wild Girl, Wild Boy*, a play about a grief-stricken girl, Elaine, who finds solace in remembering the times she spent with her father in their allotment before his death. Elaine's father had encouraged her to savor the luxuriant wildness of his unkempt plot, and she eventually conjures a Wild Boy out of a "fairy seed." Elaine sometimes has trouble distinguishing between reality and her imagination, and her mind sometimes transforms her bedroom into the allotment. Her mother is sympathetic with her daughter's grief, but seems unable to help her. A man with a nearby allotment, McNamara, had always frowned upon the wildness of Elaine's father's allotment, and now he believes that Elaine needs to be tamed as well. Elaine resists his efforts, though, and eventually she is able to help her mother see Wild Boy and experience the wildness that is the unbridled imagination.

As Rosemary Ross Johnston has noted, *Wild Girl, Wild Boy* contains two devices that connect it with the idea of the carnivalesque, as described by Mikhail Bakhtin.[2] For one thing, the play begins with a reference to the writing of the story: Elaine is in her bedroom trying to write the words of her story, but, as she says, she has "problems . . . writing" (11). Not a very good student in school, Elaine is more like Blake's bird who, born for joy, cannot sit in a cage and sing. In her resistance to formal education, Elaine shares a kinship with Mina in *Skellig* and, as we shall see, with Joe Maloney in *Secret Heart*. Elaine's true home is the "wildness of the creative imagination."[3] The Wild Boy that she conjures is, according to Johnston, a carnival figure straight out of the Roman Saturnalia.[4] The chorus of voices display the kind of heteroglossia Bakhtin describes as characteristic of the carnival.[5] This chorus reflects the disapproving voices of various teachers, students, and neighbors, but they also represent the cognitive dissonance that Elaine experiences between the world of the imagination and the "real" world in which she must live. On one level, *Wild Girl, Wild Boy* is a powerful evocation of a child's grief and an insightful analysis of the defense mechanisms she develops to deal with that pain. On another level, though, it portrays the disjunction between the Romantic emphasis on the creative imagination, as represented by Elaine and her father, and the Enlightenment emphasis on rationality, as represented by McNamara and the Chorus. The final scene of the play suggests that the imagination has won out over reason, for McNamara leaves while Elaine and her mother move into the wilderness with Wild Boy.

The play opened on February 21, 2001, at Lyric Theatre, Hammersmith, London, with Michael Dalton directing and Janet Bamford playing Elaine. In the months that followed, the production toured the country, appearing in a number of towns, including Almond's own Newcastle.

Secret Heart

Secret Heart, Almond's fourth novel for young adults, is in many ways his most mystical.[6] As he did in *Heaven Eyes*, he focuses on people marginalized by society, and he shows that, while birth ties are important, family may also be where you find it. As he did in *Skellig*, he once again uses Blakean allusions to call attention to children's ability to recognize the integration of the magical into the realities of everyday life. The physical world of the novel is a familiar one in Almond's works—a ragged English town on the fringes of civilization appropriately named "Helmouth," suggesting its affinity with the mouth of Hell. Amid the gritty reality of this setting is a veritable smorgasbord of magical phenomena, including shape-shifting, totemism, pantheism, clairvoyance, and reincarnation. As in Almond's previous works, *Secret Heart* explores the close connection between the mystical world and the natural, primitive world and shows this "merging of realms," as Wendy B. Faris describes it,[7] as fundamental to the developing identity of its adolescent protagonist.

The novel tells the story of Joe Maloney, a shy, stuttering boy who is being raised by his loving, working-class mother. He does not like school and has few friends, but his head is filled with visions of winged creatures and fairy-like beings. His one friend, Stanny Mole, and a young man named Joff want to toughen Joe up and make him into a man. By this, they mean that they want to take him out into the wilderness and teach him how to kill animals. Joe, however, resists their efforts because he is repelled by their savagery. As the novel opens, Joe is dreaming of a tiger who comes to visit him in his bedroom. The next day, he notices, to his great surprise, that a shabby circus has come to town, and he intuitively makes a connection between their arrival and his dream. Soon thereafter he is befriended by Corinna, a girl about his age, who is a trapeze artist in the circus and who claims that she and Joe share a psychic connection, perhaps having been twins in a former life. Corinna introduces Joe to the adults in the circus, including Nanty Solo, the blind soothsayer, and Hackenschmidt, the massive wrestler and circus owner. Nanty identifies Joe as the boy they have been searching for, the one who can take the skin of the circus's last tiger back into the woods and release its soul. Joe does so and in the process almost becomes the tiger. In the final scene, Joe and his mother entertain Corinna and the other circus folk in the garden of their modest home. Through his experiences, Joe has discovered not only his "secret tiger heart," but also an extended family among the people of the circus.

Coming on the heels of Almond's much praised, but less mystical, earlier works, *Secret Heart* received mixed reviews. Michael Cart, writing in his starred review in *Booklist*, lauded the novel's "heartbreaking yearning and powerful symbols" along with its scenes of "breathtaking beauty, wonder, and astonishment."[8] Paula Rohrlick, in *KLIATT Review*, described the novel as telling an "affecting, mysterious, and poetic story" that "casts a spell over the reader."[9] Sherrie Williams praised Almond for writing "a very different coming-of-age story," while successfully "avoiding the clichés that often inhabit books in this genre."[10] And Vicki Arkoff enthusiastically stated, "This is David Almond's fourth home run hit."[11] But even some of the enthusiastic reviewers found the magical elements and the symbolism to be a bit heavy-handed. Here is Arkoff again: "The inherent messages lack subtlety occasionally . . . "[12] Likewise, the reviewer for *Kirkus Reviews* worried that many readers would have trouble relating to the "largely metaphysical tale" with its "mainly symbolic characters."[13] Elaine Bearden felt that the plot was too "ethereal," and that it "lack[ed] the drive to carry its esoteric elements to novel length."[14] *The Horn Book* reviewer was less kind, describing the story as "overwrought" and "self-indulgent," and complaining that "like a taxidermied beast, there's no real *heart* at the novel's center" (emphasis in original).[15]

To be sure, this novel is something of a departure for Almond. This is his only novel to date that features third-person limited narration; all of his other works are narrated by their protagonists. This is also his most magical novel to date. Admittedly, the density of magical elements in *Secret Heart* perhaps do make the novel less than entirely successful, and no doubt it is hard for some readers to identify with the novel's "extraordinary" protagonist. Still, Almond's achievement in this, his most allegorical novel, is considerable and illustrative of his continuing development as a writer. In analyzing *Secret Heart* we can see clear connections to Almond's previous works, in terms of structure, character, imagery, and theme.

While the structure of *Heaven Eyes* emphasizes the spatial dimension in its depiction of the children's journey from Whitegates to the Black Middens and back to Whitegates again, the structure of *Secret Heart* focuses on the temporal dimension in its depiction of the three final days of the circus: Friday, Saturday, and Sunday. This three-day period parallels the Christian cycle of Christ's death, burial, and resurrection, but the allusions are oblique rather than exact, suggesting that Almond may be offering an alternative rather than a parallel to the Christian story. For Joe Maloney, Friday is a day of confrontation and choice. It begins and ends with his dreaming of a tiger coming into his bedroom, staring into his eyes, and then retreating into the darkness. In between his dreams, Joe meets two people who represent alternate ways of interacting with the world and, for Joe, alternate destinies. He meets Corinna Finch, the young trapeze artist who claims that she and Joe were once twins. Later, while hiding from the other children who are tormenting him, he encounters Joff, who offers to teach Joe how to survive by teaching him how to kill. Saturday is a day of revelation and transformation. Instead of going out with Joff and Stanny Mole, Joe once again visits the circus, where Corinna symbolically transforms him by painting his face to look like a tiger's face. He then learns from Nanty Solo and Hackenschmidt that, because of his special ability, his secret heart, he has been chosen to return the skin of the circus's last tiger to the forest. That night, Joe is once again transformed into the tiger, and he and Corinna escort the animal's soul into the Silver Forest. Sunday, then, is a day of rejuvenation. Joe and Corinna return to the circus, which is now being dismantled, the last performance now completed. Joe's mother invites Joe and his new friends to her garden for lunch. There the circus folk perform once again, but this time it is not to the jeers of a hostile crowd as it has been for a long time, but to the cheers of enthralled children. Joe transforms himself into the tiger yet again, symbolizing to all the witnesses how profoundly he has been changed in just a short time. As the day comes to a close, his mother expresses a conviction that they will all find a "lovely life" (198) tomorrow.

As in *Kit's Wilderness* and *Heaven Eyes*, the setting of *Secret Heart* takes on mythic dimensions. Joe spends much of his time in the wasteland, a place characterized by grim names that hint at "old stories, lethal games, awful discoveries. The Field of Skulls, the Ratty Paddocks, the Lostleg Railway, the Blood Pond, Adder Lane" (14). It is here, in the ruined church known as the "Blessed Chapel," that Joe enacts his personal ritual of asking God to protect his mother, the larks, and the tigers. It is here that he dreams of walking in the Silver Forest, the "enticing land beyond" (15) the boundaries of the motorway. And it is here that Joe often transforms himself—whether literally or in his imagination is hard to say—into various animals, such as skylarks, bats, weasels, snakes, and foxes. Joe is not the only character in this wasteland associated with animals: Joff has a snakeskin tattoo, Stanny Mole burrows like his animal namesake, Corinna is speckled like a skylark, and Hackenschmidt roars like a caged lion. The wasteland, then, illustrates a key characteristic of magical realism in that it is a liminal territory where two different realms often merge: "[Joe] knew how the lives of people and the lives of beasts could merge out here in the wasteland" (65).

On the edge of this wasteland sits Hackenschmidt's circus tent. Like the Blessed Chapel, the circus tent represents to Joe a place set apart, a place of magic, with a faded blue sky and sun, moon, and stars painted on the canvas. As Nanty Solo explains, the circus tent represents circumscribed wildness: it is a boundary placed around the wild beasts that were tamed by the circus's founders. At one time, it symbolized a new world, but now, much like the Blessed Chapel, it has fallen into disrepair and is awaiting its final collapse. The circus is set apart from the town as a kind of "Other," and yet the townspeople feel strangely drawn to it as well, even if just to gawk and mock. In that sense, the novel implies a contrast between the circus and the town. However, the novel does not really concern itself with the town; instead most of the scenes shift among various magical settings: the circus tent, the Blessed Chapel, the Silver Forest, and the garden of Joe's mother's house. Every place has mystical connotations, every setting magical possibilities. When Joe and Corinna go to the Black Bone Crags to entomb the head of the panther that Joff and Stanny Mole have killed, Joe notices that this natural setting is "just like the t-tent" (166) with its walls of crags and trees, and the moon and stars in the canopy above. The parallels suggest the close connection between the magic of the circus and the magic of the natural, primitive world, both of which stand in sharp contrast to the mundane reality of the civilized world as represented by the town.

Another key to understanding the idea of the circus tent as circumscribed wildness is found in Almond's "Afterword" to the published version of *Wild Girl, Wild Boy*. The passage is striking and is worth quoting at length:

> Any good story, no matter how controlled it appears on the page, is not a tame trapped thing. It still has wildness in it, a yearning to break free of its neat lines and numbered pages. And it does break free. It leaps from the page, and moves far beyond the control of the author, as soon as a reader begins to read it.
>
> . . . A story is a living thing that escapes from the page and races and prowls through our imagination.[16]

And, in an article in *The Times*, Almond echoed this theme and made the connection to young people: "Like good books, children are only superficially civilized. They want to know what lies beyond the ordinary facade. . . . And books can help to take them there."[17] The circus tent in *Secret Heart*, then, may also be seen to represent the creative imagination, and in that sense, it is like the wilderness of *Wild Girl, Wild Boy*. In taking the tiger's spirit from the circus and returning it to the Silver Forest, Joe may be symbolically releasing the power of the imagination into the world. It is appropriate, then, that the tiger returns at the end of the novel when Joe is performing his transformation in the garden.

Almond populates his magical (and metaphorical) settings with the most extraordinary cast of characters in any of his novels. In one sense, Joe Maloney is a realistically portrayed "damaged" child, much like the children in *Heaven Eyes*. His mother is poor and single; his father was a Tilt-a-Whirl operator for a traveling carnival, who left before Joe was born. Had Joe's mother been a different person, Joe might have ended up at a place like Whitegates. Joe is also an outsider, ostracized by the other children who taunt him by singing "Only Maloney" whenever he comes near. Like Mina, he finds formal education to be confining and demeaning, and he often skips school. Like the children of Whitegates, he has been examined and prodded by a parade of professionals, from psychiatrists and social workers to policemen and truant officers. Not accepted by his peers, he has stubbornly resisted socialization by adults. As in *Heaven Eyes*, the implication is that society does not, and perhaps cannot, adequately meet the needs of certain marginalized children.

Unlike the children of Whitegates, though, Joe does have a loving, nurturing mother, who recognizes early on that Joe feels things more deeply than most people. Indeed, Joe is an extraordinary child, a sensitive boy with one green eye and one brown eye, who, in his capacity to see visions, displays a spiritual kinship with William Blake. We have already seen Almond's fascination with the connection between Blake and children's heightened perceptions in *Skellig*'s multiple allusions to Blake and his poetry. The Blakean allusions are more oblique in *Secret Heart*, but no less powerful. Like Blake, Joe, even as a small child, saw faeries and beasts in his mother's garden. He has always been able to see winged creatures flying on the horizon—and, like Blake, he has made sketches of these magical visions. It is this magical sensibility, if you will, that allows Joe to dream the tiger, to ultimately become the tiger. Joe's dream and his metamorphosis recall Blake's poem "The Tyger," from *Songs of Innocence and of Experience*:

> Tyger! Tyger! burning bright
> In the forests of the night,
> What immortal hand or eye
> Could frame thy fearful symmetry?[18]

Joe's love for the darkness and the intensity of his secret heart further connect him with both the tiger of the novel and the Tyger of the poem. In a more general sense, the allusion to this particular collection of Blake's poems serves to suggest Joe's evolution from innocence to experience, an evolution effectively symbolized by the narrative's movement from Joe's dream *about* the tiger in the opening scene to his transformation *into* the tiger in the final scene.

Long before he dreams of the tiger, though, Joe has been a shape-shifter, often transforming himself into various animals. As a motif in the novel, shape-shifting suggests Joe's connection to the primitive, natural world and to the mystical realm, and it also serves as a metaphor for the fluidity of identity. Ironically, we are told early in the novel that Joe does not know how "to grow and change" (56). What this means, of course, is that he does not know how to become a man. However, his dream of and subsequent transformation into a tiger signals a significant change in his psyche and serves as an outward manifestation of his spiritual and psychological growth. The tiger is a multivalent symbol, suggesting Joe's inner strength and courage as well as the magical sensibility he shares with William Blake.

Other characters in the novel are mystical too and, it might be argued, even allegorical. Joff, for example, with his snakeskin tattoo, gold teeth, and ability to breathe fire, represents a demonic force bent on destruction. He promises to make Joe into a man by teaching him how to kill. While Joff's protégé, Stanny Mole, is initially blind to the evil and destruction that he embodies, Joe is not. He worries obsessively that Joff might be his real father, and, indeed, Joff has made overtures to Joe's mother. In a classic illustration of the Oedipal conflict, Joe dreams that the tiger, which, of course, is partly a projection of himself, is at Joff's throat. At the same time, there is a part of him that believes he should follow Joff into the wilderness and allow Joff to transform him into a man. Joe's obsession with and loathing for Joff suggests, among other things, that he may fear that he has the potential to become Joff or at least to fall under Joff's spell as his friend Stanny Mole has done. The fact that the name "Joff" is so close to "Joe" reinforces the idea that Joff may represent not just evil in the general sense, but also more specifically a part of Joe's nature. Corinna Finch, in contrast, the young trapeze artist, is associated with a kind of primitive goodness. Both her name and her talent associate her with birds, which, at least in Blake's cosmos, represent innocence and freedom. Corinna claims that she and Joe were connected in a previous life and perhaps were even twins. Indeed, they are similar, as is evident in that Joe often takes pleasure in transforming himself into a skylark. Furthermore, Corinna also has the capacity to see the winged creatures that Joe sees, and she has a deep respect for all living things. She also possesses a generative power, as is suggested by the parallel between the white speckles on the skylark eggshell that Joe finds and the white speckles on Corinna's face. As such, she clearly represents an alternative to the forces of destruction as embodied in Joff. For Joe, she represents the better part—we might even say the angelic part—of himself.

The other circus folk have both magical and allegorical functions too. Nanty Solo is the blind prophet of myth and legend, who, though she cannot see the physical world, has great insight into the spiritual realm. She serves as both historian and prophet, telling the story of the circus's genesis and foretelling its final demise. It is she who interprets Joe's dream and tells him of his destiny to take the skin of the dead tiger into the forest. Acting as high priestess of a mysterious rite, she gives Joe a bit of tiger bone to eat, thus fortifying him for the task that lies ahead. Hackenschmidt, the circus owner, has mystical and allegorical functions as well. A strong and powerful wrestler, he is also a gentle giant. His act involves his being wheeled into the circus ring in a cage and then fending off anyone in the audience who is brave enough to challenge him. Known as the "Lion of Russia," he may remind us of Aslan in C. S. Lewis's *Chronicles of Narnia*, who, though powerful enough to vanquish all foes, sacrifices himself for the greater good. Hackenschmidt is also connected with the spiritual world. As he reveals to Joe, he has shared Joe's dream of the tiger. In fact, as it turns out, Hackenschmidt is the dark figure in Joe's dream who calls the tiger back into the night.

While some of the characters in the novel are connected to the spiritual world, others clearly are not. For example, after Joff has killed the panther, he is stalked by the tiger, but he sees and hears nothing. When his accomplice, Stanny Mole, senses the tiger's presence and expresses his fear, Joff rejects him as a being a baby and sends him home. Joff remains unaware even as the tiger circles closer and closer. In that respect, he is like Bleak Winters, Joe's humanities teacher. Joe recalls seeing Winters once peering through binoculars, scoffing at a seventh grader who could see winged creatures on the horizon. Joe reflects that, while he himself can feel the lark and the tiger inside of him, "Bleak Winters was never anything else except Bleak Winters" (43). Even the name suggests the barrenness of the man's existence.

Children, on the other hand, do have the capacity to see, as is demonstrated time and again in the novel. In addition to Joe and Corinna, there is the child who tries to point out the flying creatures to Bleak Winters. There is also a child in a passing car whose startled expression indicates that she clearly has seen the tiger walking with Joe and Corrina. And Stanny Mole, although seduced by Joff's promises of manhood, has not yet lost his ability to see magical creatures. Unlike Joff, he is able to sense the tiger's presence, and this sensibility leads him to repent for having helped kill the panther. And even some adults have retained their capacity to sense the magic in the world. Nanty Solo and Hackenschmidt are clearly connected to the mystical realm. But even Joe's mother demonstrates a degree of connectedness: after Joe and Corinna return from the Silver Forest, Joe's mother tells her son that she has dreamed of tigers, and Joe embraces her, circling his arms around "the great spaces where her larks flew and her wild beasts prowled" (188).

Thematically, the novel connects this capacity to see with not only the mystical realm, but also the primitive world of nature. One typical function of magical realism is to invert the terms in a narrative equation. In *Secret Heart* that inversion of terms is evident in the dichotomy between civilization and the savagery. The savage beasts are shown to be beautiful, powerful, and even noble, while certain of the so-called civilized people prove to be the real savages. Joff and Stanny Mole kill the panther and cut off its head. This scene takes place at the exact same time as the townspeople are beating and kicking Hackenschmidt. Both Hackenschmidt and the panther are sacrificial victims, symbolizing the (temporary) ascendancy of civilization over primitivism. But Joe and Corinna's ritualistic actions of burying the panther and releasing the tiger into the forest suggest that they have the power, as Hackenschmidt says, to restore the world by returning the primitive to its rightful place.

The novel also posits a dichotomy between "real" magic and pseudo-magic. One obvious example of pseudo-magic is the photograph of unicorns that Joe sees in the circus tent. Corinna explains to him that Hackenschmit created the unicorns by removing the two horn buds from kid goats and transplanting a single horn bud onto their heads. He eventually had to destroy them because the world proved to be too harsh a place for such beauty. These fake unicorns stand in dramatic contrast to the unicorns that Joe has seen since he was a small child. But the juxtaposition of the two "versions" of unicorns in the narrative raises unsettling doubts in the reader's mind, a common effect of magical realist fiction.

Hackenschmidt's surgical skill transforms the ordinary into the extraordinary, but Joe's visions suggest an even more extraordinary version of reality. Where, the reader wonders, does reality end and the ineffable begin? A similar unease occurs in reading the passage that describes Joe's ritual in the Blessed Chapel. His rubbing the name of God on the ancient engraving, dropping a button into a crack in the floor, and intoning "our men, our men" for "amen, amen" constitute a parody of the Christian ritual—but it is not intended by Joe as a parody. He is deadly serious, and his close connection to the spiritual world lends credence to his actions. Again, the familiar is made strange in such a way that the reader is presented with an alternate version of reality and is left questioning previous preconceptions.

Parental roles are defamiliarized too—or at least transformed in various ways. With the exception of Joe's mother, there are no "traditional" parents in the novel. As stated earlier, Joe does not know his father, a carnival ride operator who saw Joe's mother as nothing more than a one-night stand. Joe fears that Joff might be his father although Joe's mother assures him that is not the case. Corinna too does not know her father, and she does not live with her mother. Her mother, a brilliant trapeze artist, has returned to Russia to teach young trapeze artists whom she apparently considers to be more gifted than her daughter. Corinna's "real" parents are Nanty Solo and Hackenschmidt. And Stanny Mole, we are told, was sent to Helmouth to live with his mother, suggesting that he too has no father. In addition to lost parents, there are lost children too. Poor Charley Caruso has lost his son Tomasso in a freak accident. Half mad with grief, he continues to call out for Tomasso, believing he sees his son in the face of every boy he meets. When he first meets Joe, he thinks Tomasso has finally returned to him. Wilfred, who is described as "dainty" by the narrator and called a "poof" by the older children, treats his dancing dogs as if they are his children. Family, it would seem, is indeed where one finds it and, moreover, is just as fluid as identity.

As we have already noted, Joe's shape-shifting indicates just how fluid identity can be. Corinna complicates this notion for Joe when she suggests that Joe may actually be Tomasso reincarnated. In fact, everyone, she says, may be someone else. She claims that she and Joe are "twins," connected somehow in a previous life. But this plethora of possible identities, while perhaps disturbing to the reader, does not seem to bother Joe and Corinna. If anything, it heightens their sense of connectedness—to each other, to the natural world, and to the realm of magic. Hackenschmidt alludes to the magical possibilities that await Joe and Corinna when he says that they have the capacity to "'refresh the world'" (109). Joe and Corinna come to understand this more fully through their experience of returning the tiger's soul to the forest and burying the panther. When Joe sees a piece of a skylark eggshell lying on the ground, he thinks of the miraculous transformation that has occurred within that egg. He also knows that he has undergone a similar miraculous transformation, and he proclaims to Corinna, "'We can d-do anything! We can g-go anywhere!'" (182). Indeed, the novel emphasizes the magical potential inside of Joe and Corinna—and by extension inside of all of the children with the capacity to "see." This is the message at the heart of *Secret Heart.*

The final scene of the novel, which takes place in Joe and his mother's garden, emphasizes the power of such a capacity to see. Much like the ending of *Wild Girl, Wild Boy*, this scene represents reconciliation, transformation, and regeneration. The final public performance of the circus has taken place on Saturday night, the tiger has been escorted back to the forest, and Joe and Corinna have returned from their night of adventure. It is now Sunday morning—the Last Day of the circus—and Joe's mother invites the performers to her house for a simple lunch. As Joe, Corinna, and the other performers make their way to the house, the older children of the town call insults after them, but many of the younger children have expressions of delight on their faces. Later, these younger children approach the garden, hoping to get a glimpse of the performers. The implication is clear: these younger children have not yet been so corrupted as to lose their capacity for wonder. They have the potential to see beyond surface realities, and they are rewarded for their curiosity. Corinna, Hackenschmidt, and Wilfred and his trained dogs take turns performing for the children, even inviting the children to participate in the acrobatics. Unencumbered by prejudice and fear, these children are able to "'[j]ump with [their] minds'" (194), as Hackenschmidt says. This is, it would seem, the last performance for the circus, but there is promise for rejuvenation, as represented by Joe and Corinna and the other children. The scene also suggests the fulfillment of a promise. As Joe's mother remarks, the odd assortment of people and animals in the garden are "'just like those tales [Joe] used to jabber come to life'" (191). And a bit later they both see "shifting shapes . . . and other half-seen things, half-known" (197) things in the grass, much like the pictures Joe drew as a young child. The visions Joe saw years ago now have been given a corporeal reality. The scene also represents a merging of the ordinary world, as represented by Joe, his mother, and the town's children, and the extraordinary world of the circus,[19] resulting in a world in which the magical and the real become intermingled.

The theme of transformation is underscored in several ways. For one thing, there is an almost Eucharistic quality to the simple meal that Joe and his mother share with the performers, suggesting again the themes of transformation and regeneration. Nanty Solo places a unicorn's tooth on Stanny Mole's tongue and implores him to eat and to "'feel [it] at work inside yourself'" (195). She goes on to explain: "'For all of us can be transformed'" (195). Joe wonders in what ways Joff will be transformed by his night in the forest. No one, however, has been transformed more obviously than Joe himself, as his mother indicates when she says, "'[L]ook at you now. Listen to you now'" (194). Furthermore, Joe's transformation, it is implied, has the potential to transform the world. He is the last to perform on this Last Day, with Corinna urging him on, saying, "'Do it, Joe. . . . Refresh the world'" (197). His performance is to once again become the tiger, to prowl and claw and leap, and in so doing to summon the tiger's spirit, for a brief moment, from the forest. Joe's mother's statement that she and Joe will find a "'lovely life'" (198) tomorrow is echoed by Nanty Solo, who says that this will be true for all of them. The Last Day, according to Nanty, may just be when "'the first of all days'" (194) is discovered. The final image is one of overwhelming affirmation, in that, even as the sun goes down on the garden scene, they know that "[t]he world beneath them turned toward day" (199) and toward the promise of a transcendent future.

Kate, the Cat and the Moon

To date, Almond has written one picture book, *Kate, the Cat and the Moon*, although he says that he has plans to write additional books in that format.[20] *Kate, the Cat and the Moon* with pictures by the award-winning illustrator Stephen Lambert, tells the story of a little girl who wakes up one night and hears a cat meowing outside of her window. Kate responds with her own "meow" and then is transformed into a cat. She then bounds down the stairs, out the door, and into the garden where she meets the cat who has called to her. They go off exploring, through gardens, down lanes, across fields, and into magical dreams. Once the adventure is over and the stars begin to fade out, Kate returns home, and, as she reaches her bed, she is transformed once more into a little girl. The next morning over breakfast, Kate's family talk about their dreams, which parallel the dreams that Kate observed in the nighttime romp.

Julia Eccleshare, writing in *The Guardian*, admired Almond's "poetic text" and Lambert's "painterly illustrations," and she praised the book as a rare picture book that "entertains through wonder rather than high drama."[21] Nicolette Jones, reviewing the book for *The Sunday Times*, also noted the poetic quality of the text and found that the pastel illustrations "share the suggestiveness and gentleness of Almond's text." The result, she found, was a book that "takes the 'Was it all a dream?' formula and makes it into something new and imaginative."[22]

We can see in this story the familiar elements of magical realism—dreams, transformations, and a fascination with the primitive. In some ways, the story recalls Maurice Sendak's *Where the Wild Things Are* in its depiction of a child's journey into the wilderness of the imagination and then back home again. Kate's journey, though, seems less psychological and more imaginative than Max's. As the story opens, she is not being punished for having acted wildly, and, when she returns at the end, there is no emotional reconciliation. Indeed, there was no initial rupture. Instead, Kate's journey is presented as the most natural thing in the world, and is clearly indicative of her powerful imagination. As he has done in so many of his works, Almond once again pays tribute to the special ability of children to see the magic in the world around them—and their ability to transform themselves into anything they want to be. Still, in her exuberant foray into the wilds of her own imagination, Kate proves in many ways to be a sister to Max.

Notes

1. David Almond, "Afterword," *Wild Girl, Wild Boy: A Play* (London: Hodder Children's Books, 2002) 84–85.

2. Rosemary Ross Johnston, "Carnivals, the Carnivalesque, *The Magic Puddin'*, and David Almond's *Wild Girl, Wild Boy*: Toward a Theorizing of Children's Plays," *Children's Literature in Education* 34.2 (2003): 141–45.

3. Johnston, "David Almond's *Wild Girl, Wild Boy*," 142.

4. Johnston, "David Almond's *Wild Girl, Wild Boy*," 143.

5. Johnston, "David Almond's *Wild Girl, Wild Boy*," 142.

6. In the late fall of 2002, a stage production of *Secret Heart* was mounted at the Royal Exchange Theatre, Manchester. Amanda Dalton adapted the book, and Wils Wilson directed. Almond himself was not directly involved in the production. Reviews were mixed. Jeremy Kingston, for example, said that the book had "dispelled [his] anti-circus prejudice" and that the play and the cast "[did] not disappoint." Dominic Cavendish, however, was "befuddled" by the play, which he described as "a clodhopping stage adaptation" of the novel. See Jeremy Kingston, rev. of *Secret Heart: The Play*, adap. Amanda Dalton, *The Times* [London] 12 December 2002, *NewsBank*, online, 1 September 2005; and Dominic Cavendish, "Tiger without Teeth Stalks a Shattered Dreamscape," rev. of *Secret Heart: The Play*, adap. Amanda Dalton, *The Daily Telegraph* [London] 12 December 2002, *NewsBank*, online, 1 September 2005.

7. Wendy B. Faris, *Ordinary Enchantments: Magical Realism and the Remystification of Narrative* (Nashville, TN: Vanderbilt University Press, 2004) 21–23.

8. Michael Cart, rev. of *Secret Heart*, by David Almond, *Booklist* 99.3 (2002), *Children's Literature Reviews*, *Children's Literature Comprehensive Database*, online, 11 March 2005.

9. Paula Rohrlick, rev. of *Secret Heart*, by David Almond, *KLIATT Review* 36.6 (2002), *Children's Literature Reviews*, *Children's Literature Comprehensive Database*, online, 11 March 2005.

10. Sherrie Williams, rev. of *Secret Heart*, by David Almond, *VOYA* 25.5 (2002), *Children's Literature Reviews*, *Children's Literature Comprehensive Database*, online, 11 March 2005.

11. Vicki Arkoff, rev. of *Secret Heart*, by David Almond, *Midwest Book Review* March 2003, *Children's Literature Reviews*, *Children's Literature Comprehensive Database*, online, 11 March 2005.

12. Arkoff, rev. of *Secret Heart*.

13. Rev. of *Secret Heart*, by David Almond, *Kirkus Reviews* 70.17 (2002), *Children's Literature Reviews*, *Children's Literature Comprehensive Database*, online, 11 March 2005.

14. Elaine A. Bearden, rev. of *Secret Heart*, by David Almond, *Bulletin of the Center for Children's Books* 56.4 (2002), *Children's Literature Reviews*, *Children's Literature Comprehensive Database*, online, 11 March 2005.

15. Rev. of *Secret Heart*, by David Almond, *Horn Book Guide* 14.1 (2003), *Children's Literature Reviews*, *Children's Literature Comprehensive Database*, online, 11 March 2005.

16. Almond, "Afterword," 88.

17. David Almond, "Magic All Around If You Only Know How to Look," *The Times* [London] 6 August 2003, *NewsBank*, online, 1 September 2005.

18. William Blake, "The Tyger," *The Complete Poetry and Prose of William Blake*, ed. by David V. Erdman (New York: Anchor Books, 1988) ll. 1–4.

19. Kit Spring, rev. of *Secret Heart*, by David Almond, *The Observer* [London] 11 March 2001, *Guardian Unlimited*, online, 26 August 2005, http://books.guardian.co.uk/reviews/roundupstory/0,,449761,00.html.

20. David Almond, personal interview, 21 April 2005.

21. Julia Eccleshare, "Julia Eccleshare's Picture-Book Roundup," rev. of *Kate, the Cat and the Moon*, by David Almond, illus. Stephen Lambert, *The Guardian* [London] 13 November 2004, *NewsBank*, online, 1 September 2005.

22. Nicolette Jones, rev. of *Kate, the Cat and the Moon*, by David Almond, illus. Stephen Lambert, *The Sunday Times* [London] 24 October 2004, *NewsBank*, online, 1 September 2005.

CHAPTER SEVEN

~

At the Gates of Hell: *The Fire-Eaters*

As a number of reviewers noted, *The Fire-Eaters* is an anti-war novel. Indeed, Almond acknowledged in his acceptance speech for the Boston Globe–Horn Book Award for Fiction and Poetry that he began writing the book at the same time the buildup to the war with Iraq was starting, a time when "[w]ords like *war* and *bomb* and *threat* were being used with dreadful abandon."[1] These war cries caused him to recall a similar time during his childhood when he, his family, and friends experienced the threat of world annihilation: the Cuban Missile Crisis. Thus it was that he came to choose this particular time period, the autumn of 1962, as the backdrop for his story of a working-class adolescent boy's coming of age and his encounter with a battle-scarred fire-eater.

As the novel opens, Bobby Burns and his mother are visiting the outdoor market in Newcastle, when they see a crowd gathered around a man who is balancing a cart wheel on his forehead. This man, it turns out, is McNulty, a fire-eater and escapologist who served with Bobby's dad in Burma during World War II. His mind damaged by the war, McNulty now spends his days insisting that people pay to watch him engage in acts of self-mutilation. Bobby's first encounter with the fire-eater occurs just as a number of changes are occurring in Bobby's life. For one thing, he is about to begin his studies at Sacred Heart School, a middle-class Catholic school to which he has won admission through his academic achievement. As a result of starting this new school, he is going to be separated from his longtime working-class friends Joseph Connor, who will be attending the local trade school, and Ailsa Spink, the sea coaler's daughter, who has been admitted to Sacred Heart but prefers to stay at home and take care of her father and brothers. Bobby also meets the new boy in town, Daniel Gower, who is an outsider partly because he comes from a different part of England (Kent) and partly because his parents are not working class; in fact, they are teachers at the local university. As a result, Daniel and his parents tend to view the inhabitants of Keely Bay as backward and even violent. When Bobby and Daniel start to school, they immediately become the victims of a sadistic teacher. They eventually resist this tyrrany by secretly distributing incriminating pictures of the teacher throughout the school. This autumn proves to be a time of turmoil for Bobby, for, in addition to having to deal with a tyrant at school, he is having to deal with his father's mysterious illness at home, and with the mounting tensions between the United States and Russia in the world at large. In addition, McNulty moves into the dunes near Bobby's house, and Bobby and Ailsa begin to care for him by taking him food and blankets. One night, at the height of the Cuban Missile Crisis, Bobby, his friends, and their families gather on the beach to build a bonfire and await the apocalypse. McNulty, in the act of performing his fire-breathing, breathes the fire into himself and dies. The anticipated apocalypse never comes, of course, and the ultimate message of the novel is one of hope rather than despair. Specifically, it suggests that, through the love and support of family and friends, one can fight tyranny wherever one might find it.

A number of reviewers praised *The Fire-Eaters* for its lyrical evocation of character, place, and history. Susanna Coghlan, for instance, described the novel as a "warmly atmospheric" work that leaves the reader "with an intense feeling of satisfaction and a desire to explore, to experience and to enjoy this strange world which Almond so vividly and lovingly presents."[2] Ilene Cooper felt that Almond had returned to "some familiar themes—the mystery and pain of life" in creating a book in which "everyday detail mingles with the grotesque." She goes on to say that, while not all of the characters are "well integrated" into the story, the overall effect is "so imaginative and layered that turning the pages is always meaningful."[3] Debra Nelson felt that Almond was quite successful in integrating the "many events and characters" so that "everything seems to fit."[4] *The Horn Book* reviewer too applauded Almond for his ability to present "themes [that] are tightly woven through the story, holding together pieces large and small."[5] The reviewer for *Kirkus Reviews* characterized the novel as "moody and layered" with "dark, dramatic threads" running throughout.[6] Nicolette Jones, writing for *The Sunday Times*, praised the novel for its "mix of realism, imagination and emotion," and Amanda Craig described the book as a "beautiful and brilliant novel," one that "crackles with passion, humor and the possibility of the sublime."[7] Although more than one reviewer found the the connection between the Cuban Missile Crisis and the events of the novel to be somewhat oblique,[8] most reviewers praised Almond's skillful artistry and felt that the novel represented some of his best work. The *Kirkus* reviewer likened the book to "Almond's choicest," while Teri S. Lesesne writing for *VOYA* agreed that in *The Fire-Eaters* Almond was "in fine form."[9] Timnah Card wrote that "[t]he complex grace Almond has previously brought to his mystically touched fantasies now drives this involving anti-war novel."[10] And Jan Mark, writing for *The Guardian*, praised the novel for being "beautifully written, and polished to a lapidary gloss" and for presenting "a record of events so skilfully arranged that everything shows to advantage."[11]

The novel was named to a number of "best book" lists and won several awards, including the Nestle Smarties Book Prize Gold Winner 2003, the Whitbread Children's Book of the Year Award 2003, the Guardian Award for Children's Fiction Shortlist 2003, and the Boston Globe–Horn Book Awards Winner 2004. This was Almond's first book since *Kit's Wilderness* to win such accolades.

Though reviewers praised Almond's return to the best form of his best previous work, in some ways the novel represents a departure for him. It is, for example, his most realistic work, both in terms of time period and place. The characters speak in a northern English Geordie dialect that is more pronounced than that of the characters in his other books.[12] Also, the details of the place and the time period—Keely Bay and Newcastle—mark the book's locale as being of a distinct region during a distinct historical period. Moreover, although there is a great deal of the grotesque, especially in the character of the fire-eater, there is little actual magic in the novel, and, in fact, nothing occurs that cannot be explained rationally. Also, Almond deals more directly—and more critically—with social issues in this novel, like the debilitating effects of class distinctions, institutional abuse, nuclear proliferation, and war in general. And, finally, for the first time Almond portrays his adolescent characters as sexual beings. The sum total of these various elements, then, is a novel that can be considered much more realistic than Almond's previous works. Only the future can tell whether this signals a new trend or merely an anomaly in Almond's opus.

Extraordinary Beings

In some ways, *The Fire-Eaters* may be seen as a companion story to *Skellig*. Both novels focus on an adolescent boy who is adapting to a new environment, and both involve a special friendship between a boy and a girl who take care of an extraordinary being that seems to be connected—either literally or metaphorically—to the spiritual realm. The decrepit angel embodied in the figure of Skellig is replaced by the demonic image of McNulty the fire-eater. But McNulty is no more evil than Skellig; if anything, McNulty is a victim of evil, having been traumatized by his experiences in World War II. In both novels, the protagonist is dealing with the illness of a family member—Michael with his baby sister's heart condition, Bobby with his father's mysterious cough. In both cases, it seems that the protagonist and his friend effect the healing of their respective family members through miracles. Michael and Mina implore Skellig to heal Michael's sister, while Bobby and Ailsa pray that Bobby's father will be healed. In *Skellig*, though, the subsequent healing of the baby is attributed, at least by Michael and Mina, to Skellig's intervention, whereas Bobby is not so certain that his and Ailsa's prayers made a difference. *The Fire-Eaters*, then, is the darker of the two novels, for it not only suggests that there may be no omnipotent force in the universe, but it also shows that the ministrations of Bobby and Ailsa are not enough to save McNulty. Unlike Skellig, who flies away restored to health, McNulty is consumed by his demons, as is symbolized by his final act of breathing in fire and then dying. Both novels empower their young readers by portraying the potential of young people to effect positive change in their own lives and thus in the world. *Skellig* connects this special ability overtly to the mystical realm, while

The Fire-Eaters connects it to the more ordinary power of family, friends, and community.

To be sure, there are magical elements in *The Fire-Eaters*, and they are evident most clearly in the characters of McNulty and Ailsa. The figure of the fire-eater is one that Almond had been fascinated with for some time. He has said that the image is one he remembers from his childhood, when his grandfather took him to the market in Newcastle. This bizaare character both frightened and fascinated eight-year-old David, a character he would return to several times in his writing.[13] He used it in two of the stories in *A Kind of Heaven*, including the title story, which is similar in many respects to the opening of *The Fire-Eaters*: a boy and his mother (it is the mother, rather than the father, who is ill) encounter a half-deranged escapologist at the outdoor market in Newcastle. Like *The Fire-Eaters*, the story is set against the backdrop of the Cold War and the constant threat of nuclear annihilation. In another story in that collection, "Fiesta," a young boy is taken in by a group of fire-eaters when his mother starts spending more time with her boyfriend than with him. The image surfaces yet again in *Secret Heart* when we learn that one of Joff's habits is fire-eating. In the case of Joff and the fire-eaters in "Fiesta," the practice is clearly associated with darkness and despair. When the boy in "Fiesta" becomes a fire-eater himself, it is with a feeling of desperation that he apprentices himself to these men. But in "A Kind of Heaven" and *The Fire-Eaters*, the connotations are more complex. In both works, the fire-eater is depicted as suffering from what we would now call post-traumatic stress syndrome, having been irrevocably damaged by his experiences in World War II. This character in these two works represents not evil itself, but rather the destructive effects of evil, specifically the evil of war.

McNulty's powers are associated with magic, but they are not magical. As Bobby's father explains, McNulty spent time in Burma during the war sitting at the feet of various "magic men" and "[m]iracle makers," some of whom perhaps "could work true magic and make true miracles come to pass" (53). The implication, though, is that McNulty is not a true miracle worker, but rather a lost soul whose acts of fire-breathing and self-mutilation are a grotesque parody of the things he saw during the war. Like Miss Golightly, Loosa Fine, and Jack Law of *Counting Stars*, McNulty has been mentally and psychologically damaged by his experiences, and, because of that, he is an outcast, inspiring horror and loathing among some, sympathy and fascination among others. Both Bobby and Joseph dream of McNulty and even of becoming McNulty. Joseph has tattoos like McNulty, and he says that he wants to try fire-eating. By the end of the novel, he has decided that instead of becoming a builder like his father, he wants to be a fire-eater. Bobby too is connected with McNulty, serving as his impromptu assistant and later helping to care for him. He even imagines becoming McNulty, as he passes his hand through the flame of a candle and sticks a pin into his flesh. As Bobby does these things, he thinks about Jesus "writhing on his cross" (107) and the martyr St. Sebastian, shot through with arrows. Bobby's association of these sacrificial victims with McNulty parallels his own sacrificial nature, specifically his desire to sacrifice himself for his sick father, and it also foreshadows McNulty's final symbolic act of self-sacrifice in breathing in the fire that is threatening to engulf the world. In that sense, McNulty references the miraculous, although he himself does not possess supernatural powers.

The other character associated with magic is Ailsa Spink. In many ways, Ailsa is portrayed as an earth mother figure, taking care of her father and two brothers and rescuing a fawn who appears to be dead. She is very bright, and, in fact, has won admission to the school that Bobby and Daniel are going to. Her interests, though, are in the natural, even primitive, world rather than in formal education. She has a strong sense of self, as is evident when Bobby tells her that she should be proud of who she is: she responds fiercely that she *is* proud of who she is and for that reason wants to remain who she is. Of all of the characters in the novel, she is the one most closely associated with magic. After finding a lifeless fawn, she asks God to heal it and then spends the night dreaming of it running through fields and forests. The next morning she discovers that the fawn has its eyes open. Although her brother says that deer sometimes "play possum," Ailsa is certain that she has witnessed—and helped to facilitate—a miraculous resurrection. Later, she and Bobby pray for Bobby's father, with similar results: the test report from the hospital says that nothing is seriously wrong. These "miracles," however, can certainly be attributed to natural laws. In fact, no event or character must be interpreted as incontrovertibly magical, making this the first of Almond's works in which this is the case.

The Politics of Identity

Almond's concern is more clearly with his adolescent protagonist[14] and the changes that are occurring to him and his world. As Bobby is growing up, he is experiencing a myriad of tumultuous changes: he is starting a new school, which also signals his entrance into a new social class; he is confronted with a bullying teacher; he is forging new friendships and trying to hold on to old friendships; he has his first romantic relationship; he is facing the possible loss of his father to a mysterious illness; and he must deal with the threat of nuclear annihilation looming on the horizon. The real crux of the novel focuses on Bobby's encounters with institutional constraints of three basic types: social, as exemplified by the cultural differences between Bobby and his working-class friends, on the one hand, and the new boy, Daniel, on the other; educational, as embodied in the sadistic teacher Mr. Todd; and political, as represented by the Cold War conflict between the United States and the Soviet Union. A consideration of each of these can help us to understand how they function in the novel to contribute to Bobby's emerging identity and integration into society.

The novel's concern with class distinctions is announced early on when we learn that Bobby has been accepted to Sacred Heart School because he has performed well on an academic achievement test. His working-class parents (his father works in the local shipyard) are very proud of him, as is evident in the joy they take in seeing him in his new school uniform. His friend Joseph, who also is of working-class parents and who is three years older than Bobby, is proud of him as well and enjoys teasing him about the fact that Bobby will leave one day to go off to university and then a promising professional career. Joseph, in contrast, knows intuitively that he is stuck in his working-class existence. He says that he expects to stay in Keely Bay and become a builder like his father. While Joseph is proud of Bobby's accomplishments and opportunities, he is also wary of Bobby's budding friendship with the new boy, Daniel Gower. No doubt part of Joseph's distrust of Daniel has to do with the fact that Daniel's parents are well educated and solidly middle class; in fact, they are both teachers at the local university. But part of Joseph's antagonism toward Daniel can be attributed to what the new boy represents—someone who will potentially replace Joseph as

Bobby's best friend. That is why Joseph throws Bobby to the ground after seeing him leaving Daniel's house. Still, Bobby considers Joseph to be his best friend, and he even measures himself against his friend—both literally and figuratively, it would seem—as they are lying together in the dunes.

Daniel, for his part, seems to embody those traits that Joseph—and Bobby, to a degree—find distasteful: he is standoffish, barely acknowledging Joseph's greeting the first time they meet, and he is arrogant, often implying that the locals are ignorant and violent. When he first comes to Keely Bay, Daniel is clearly a snob, someone who deliberately sets himself apart from the other children his age. At one point, he invites Bobby home, only to insult him and his parents. Bobby measures himself against Daniel too, wondering if he could beat him in a fight. More than once he struggles to find common ground between them. Yet Bobby is also intrigued by the new boy, with his sophisticated parents who read books, drink wine, and listen to jazz. He also discovers that Daniel—whether because of his security with his social standing, his outsider status, or his particular personality—is willing to mount a subversive resistance campaign against the tyranny of Mr. Todd. As it turns out, this is the common ground that Bobby has been looking for. He offers to help Daniel distribute the photographs, and they both end up getting expelled from school. But class distinctions are a powerful force. Grace, the headmaster of the school, immediately spots Daniel as the instigator of the incriminating photographs, and he tries to use the difference between Bobby's and Daniel's social classes to plant doubt in Bobby's mind. He tells Bobby that Daniel is not really his friend and that Daniel will have many opportunities, regardless of whether he stays at Sacred Heart School, but for Bobby Sacred Heart is his only hope for entering the middle class. The comment is meant to be insidious, and Bobby, to his credit, rejects it. However, Grace's ploy illustrates the potentially debilitating power of social class distinctions.

Ailsa Spink's character serves to illustrate not only class differences, but gender inequities as well. As noted earlier, Ailsa in many ways is an earth mother figure. She is associated with generative power: she is possibly capable of effecting healing through her dreams, she cares for her father and brothers, and she helps her family eke out a living by harvesting coal from the sea. She is staunchly proud of who she is and where she comes from, and for that reason she sees no need to go to Sacred Heart School, even though she has done very well on the achievement test. To Daniel, the Spinks are primitive examples of local color. He recognizes their hardship but does not understand their humanity. Moreover, he thinks Ailsa is "stupid" for not wanting to take advantage of the opportunity to go to a good school. And, while Bobby realizes that Ailsa is far from stupid, he too does not understand her resistance to going to school (although one suspects that Mina and Joe Maloney would understand perfectly). Ailsa's brother, on the other hand, endorses his sister's decision because he sees no reason for a girl to get an education; all she will ever need, he believes, is a good man to support her. In the end, Ailsa does agree to go to school—and she turns out to be the brightest student there. In doing so, she manages to break free from both class and gender constraints imposed upon her by society. But one wonders at what cost. In many ways, Ailsa's family represents, even during the historical period in which the novel is set, a way of life that is passing away. Given Almond's generally optimistic view of all of his adolescent characters, we may hope that Ailsa will retain her connection to the primitive, mystical realm even while taking her rightful place as a full participant in society.

The Politics of Authority

A second major institutional constraint that Bobby must face is the authority of the school and, by association, the church. Sacred Heart is a Catholic school with a golden crucifix over the entrance and crucifixes over all of the interior doors. The headmaster, ironically named Grace, has both a crucifix and a statue of the Blessed Virgin Mary in his office. Almond levels some sharp criticism at institutionalized child abuse, and he never lets the reader forget that this school and, presumably this behavior, is sanctioned by the church. Indeed, this is his most overt criticism of any societal institution since the stories of *Counting Stars*, where he also portrays the abuses of church and school authorities. On the very first day of school Bobby and Daniel are strapped by Mr. Todd, a sadistic teacher who singles them out in order to make an example of them. This victimization at Todd's hands forges an initial bond between Bobby and Daniel that will grow stronger as the novel progresses and they begin to fight back with subversive tactics. This is not an isolated incident, as Todd is constantly on the prowl looking for potential offenders. When he encounters a disturbance in Miss Bute's biology class, a "cold grin" breaks across his face (94). Then, when he cannot identify the perpetrators, he chooses two sacrificial victims, one of whom is Daniel. Later, Daniel surreptitiously takes a photograph of Todd, which he enlarges, showing only Todd's giant face, "teeth bared, froth at the corners of his mouth, eyes glaring down at some unseen victim" (151). As readers, we are implicitly invited to compare McNulty's evil appearance but actual harmlessness with Todd's truly evil nature. The headmaster, Grace, is portrayed as being complicitous in Todd's abuses. Indeed, Grace uses twisted words rather than a strap to inflict his damage. When trying to ferret out those responsible for distributing the photographs, Grace assembles all of the students in the auditorium and tells them, ironically, that they are all a community and must care for one another. He then promises to "make [their] lives a hell" until he discovers the guilty parties (147). As we have already noted, once Bobby and Daniel are caught, Grace tries to turn them against each other by telling Bobby that, because Daniel is of a different social class, he will never truly be Bobby's friend.

Bobby has shown doubts about the existence of God, especially when he thinks that his prayers for his father have been heard by no one—because there is no one to hear. But he never explicitly criticizes Todd's and Grace's hypocrisy, although Almond's implicit criticism is palpable. Moreover, Bobby never turns his back on the idea of school even though it becomes a place of misery for him and all of his friends. Instead, he and Daniel find a way to resist the evil rather than be subsumed by it. To be sure, as in his other novels, Almond's criticism of the school is not total. Miss Bute, for example, is portrayed as being a kind, sensitive, and effective teacher. While demonstrating the dissection of a frog, she emphasizes that all living things are sacred. She says that, when one cuts open a frog to discover the mystery of life, "'the mystery only deepens'" (129). It is perhaps significant that immediately after this lesson Daniel vows to get revenge on Todd.

The Politics of Apocalypse

The third oppressive institutional constraint that Bobby must face is a political one, specifically the threat of nuclear holocaust occasioned by the showdown between the United States and the Soviet Union during the Cuban Missile Crisis. The specter of apocalypse—and, in broader terms, the pervasive evil of all wars—is yet another major theme of the book. Three sets of references to war are evident in the novel. One set is associated with World War II and focuses largely on Bobby's father's and McNulty's experiences in that war. Bobby's father shows his son a gas mask that was issued to everyone during the war. He also shows Bobby the photographs of his own war experiences in Burma. And he makes it clear that the war's trauma is the cause of McNulty's dementia. He admits, in fact, that the war had a debilitating effect on everyone: "'[I]t drove us all a little mad and a little sad and left us all with partly broken hearts'" (54). McNulty, then, is simply an extreme case that exemplifies the war's devastation of those who participated in it. A second set of war references involves the current events of the novel's time period, the fall of 1962. It is a time when images of Kennedy, Kruschev, missiles, and mushroom clouds dominate television screens and newspapers. McNulty, hypersensitive to the gathering storm clouds, exclaims that "'[t]he world's afire'" (160), and he equates fallout shelters with graves, suggesting that he understands more clearly than many so-called sane people the real implications of nuclear war.

The third set of references is to the war games the children play in the pines. Bobby explains that the children reenact various atrocities from history, from ancient Roman gladiatorial contests to cowboys and Indians, from the Crusades to World War II. He says that in these games "[k]ids were tortured, hanged, drawn and quartered" (37). In many ways, this scenario is the most chilling, and, as such, it works on several levels. By playing these gruesome games, the children may be attempting to defuse something that frightens them, and in that sense they are much like the children who play the game called Death in *Kit's Wilderness*. On another level their behavior reflects the insidious effects of a political climate that wants them to think of war as not merely inevitable, but even pleasurable—a fun game to be won or lost today and then fought again tomorrow. And, on yet another level, their behavior parallels the actions of government leaders who, as Daniel's father observes, are "'playing with things they don't understand'" (97).

As Roberta Seelinger Trites points out, in examining the political ideologies evident in young adult fiction, it is important to consider not only "the historical context in which the story is set," but also "the historical context in which it was written."[15] That is certainly the case with *The Fire-Eaters*, as Almond himself made clear in his Boston Globe–Horn Book Award acceptance speech. In the buildup to the war with Iraq, he said, there was a great deal of self-righteous rhetoric on both sides. In the novel, Almond does not take sides with any particular political ideology, but instead shows that the Americans and the Soviets are both at fault. In truth, it is ordinary people who are conscripted to fight a war and who suffer the most devastating effects of war. Almond's message is clear: war, under any circumstances, is hell. And, as the children's war games grimly remind us, it is often the children who suffer most.

The Politics of Images

In addition to negotiating his position with the social structures of class, school and church, and global politics, another part of Bobby's socialization process is his coming to understand the role that images can play in both exerting power on and empowering the individual. Specifically, four different groups of images play a role in Bobby's socialization and maturation. One group is associated with his father's childhood and experiences in Burma during World War II, and these photographs serve as a kind of visual analog for the process of memory, reinforcing Bobby's connections to his heritage in terms of family and place. There are, for example, photographs of his father as a little boy on the beach, another of him with Joseph's father, and one of him as a teenager with Ailsa's father. These photographs recapitulate Bobby's own life—or, to be more exact, Bobby's life is now recapitulating that of his father as a boy and teenager. There is another photograph of his mother as a young woman that is said to have had a talismanic effect on Bobby's father, protecting him from harm while he was serving in the military during World War II. And there is a photograph of Bobby's father in his army uniform, taken in Burma by a young soldier who was killed by a sniper on the same morning the photograph was taken. Trites has analyzed the role of photography within the young adult novel, arguing that "photography affords YA novelists an opportunity to explore the relationship between agency, death, and discourse."[16] The photograph not only captures the object being photographed but also implies the subject who is taking the photograph.[17] In the photograph of Bobby's father as a young soldier is implied the young soldier who was the photographer—the same young soldier who died a few hours later. In capturing the fleeting image of Bobby's father as a young man—and the "trace" of the now dead photographer—this photograph allows, indeed forces, Bobby to face the possibility of his father's death and, by extension, his own death.

Bobby also learns that images can be used, in effect, for cultural appropriation and commodification. Daniel's father's photographs of the residents of Keely Bay is a case in point. He has been photographing people that he apparently considers to be examples of "rustics," with the intention of publishing the collection in a book. That these photographs represent a cultural (mis)appropriation and a detached, even condescending objectification of Bobby and his family and friends can be seen in Daniel's comments when he shows Bobby the photograph his father has taken of Joseph: "'[My father says] you'd only get somebody like him in a place like this'" (101). When Bobby protests at having his friend objectified in such a way, Daniel's reply again betrays his middle-class prejudice: "'That's what you do up here, isn't it? Fight and scrap like animals?'" (101). Bobby is clearly disturbed by Daniel's and his father's biased view of the inhabitants of Keely Bay. It is less clear, though, whether he also sees his father's photographs of the Burmese "[f]akes and fakirs and magic men" in the same way (53), but the astute reader will notice the similarities.

A much more pervasive example of the cultural power of images is evident in the numerous images of Kennedy, Kruschev, missiles, and mushroom clouds that appear on television and in newspapers during, and in the weeks leading up to, the Cuban Missile Crisis. These images are used by both superpowers to defy one another in a frightening game of public posturing and one-upmanship. While history has shown that, in fact, both superpowers were working behind the scenes to avoid a military confrontation, the images that were widely disseminated during that time were clearly intended by each superpower to demonstrate strength and defiance in the eyes of the world and to heighten mistrust of the "enemy" by creating a sense of terror in the populace.

The Cuban Missile Crisis began, of course, over a series of photographs taken from spy planes, showing the installation of missiles in Cuba. The fact that these photographs nearly brought the world to the brink of nuclear holocaust attests to the power of images both to record and expose. It is the power of images to expose that Daniel harnesses when he takes photographs of Todd in the act of strapping a student, enlarges them to highlight the teacher's sadistic glee, and then distributes them throughout the school. If images can be manipulated in order to assert authority—and this is surely the case with the images of sword rattling propagated by the superpowers as well as the association of religious icons with school authority—then, as Daniel and Bobby demonstrate, images can also be manipulated to resist authority. The dissemination of these photographs throughout the school effectively subverts Todd's—and, by extension, the headmaster's—authority. Although Bobby and Daniel are expelled for a time, their act of resistance eventually leads Miss Bute to speak out against the atrocities that Todd has been committing. We do not know what ultimately happens to Todd, but we do know that Bobby and Daniel are reinstated in good standing. Clearly, their act of resistance has had its intended effect.

This use of images to resist unjust authority is what cements Bobby and Daniel's friendship and, symbolically, helps bring the two social classes together. Both Joseph and the Spinkses applaud Bobby for getting "chucked out" of school. Moreover, Bobby's parents and Daniel's parents discover common ground through the children. It is Daniel's father who suggests that the two boys are "fighters" because they perhaps "were brought up in similar ways" (200). Bobby's parents express pride in their son's actions, and it seems safe to assume that Daniel's parents have similar feelings. The significance of resistance also has larger implications, as is suggested by Joseph when he encourages Bobby to resist the destructive forces threatening their world: "'At least make a noise. At least say, I'm me! I'm Bobby Burns!'" (183). The novel implies that people can and should work together across social classes and cultural differences to resist unjust authority, whether that authority is in the form of bullying teachers or misguided world leaders.

The climactic scene in the novel, in which all of the characters gather on the beach in a show of solidarity and quiet defiance, in many ways parallels the climactic scene in the garden in *Secret Heart*. Whereas in *Secret Heart* the garden scene represents a commemoration of the Last Day of the circus, the beach scene in *The Fire-Eaters* marks what may be the last day of the world. In both scenes the characters, united by the common bond of their humanity, affirm life rather than give in to the forces of darkness. Although Bobby learns later that some people in Newcastle fought in the streets during the height of the crisis, the people on the beach at Keely Bay sustain one another, sharing food and drink. By their simple and very human actions, they rage (quietly) against the dying of the light, in effect, as Bobby says, "shout[ing], No!" (214). The lighting of the bonfires for an early celebration of Guy Fawkes Night[18] symbolically serves the same purpose. It is on this "last day" that McNulty gives his final performance, having been summoned by Bobby and Ailsa to the beach where the others are gathered. He has Bobby bind him with chains, he pierces his cheeks with the metal skewer, and he swallows the fire so artfully that, as with the greatest of the fire-eaters, it is hard to tell "where the fire end[s] and the man [begins]" (212). McNulty's final act proves to be one of self-sacrifice, however, as he breathes the fire into himself and dies as a result. His sacrifice does not literally save the world, of course, but it does symbolize the terrible human cost of war. It also parallels the self-sacrifice of others in the novel, especially Bobby, who prays that he will be taken and the world saved and who, along with Daniel, risks physical punishment and expulsion from school in order to expose the evils of Mr. Todd. Hence the plural nature of the book's title: McNulty is not the only fire-eater; in many ways all of the people on the beach who shout an emphatic "No" are, in varying degrees, fire-eaters too.

Ultimately, the novel functions much like the photographs that Bobby and Daniel distribute, constituting both a record of injustice and insanity and sounding a call to arms to resist such atrocities, wherever one might find them. It is significant that, late in the novel, Bobby explicitly refers to the story he is writing about this experience, and it is equally significant that, when he reveals Miss Bute's decision to speak up against the unjust authority of the school, he says that with her actions "another story started" (216). The power of images is thus paralleled by the power of narrative, a theme that recurs throughout Almond's works. Perhaps more clearly in *The Fire-Eaters* than in his earlier works, stories are shown to have not only personal redemptive power, as is the case in *Heaven Eyes*, but also socially constructive power. As Almond said so eloquently in his Boston Globe–Horn Book Award acceptance speech, "[E]ach time a story is told or written, listened to or read, an act of re-creation and of optimism occurs, the forces of destruction are repelled for a time, and the world is renewed."[19]

Notes

1. David Almond, "Fiction and Poetry Award Winner," *The Horn Book* 81.1 (2005) 35.
2. Susanna Coghlan, rev. of *The Fire-Eaters*, by David Almond, *Inis—The Magazine of Children's Books Ireland*, no. 7 (2003), *Children's Literature Reviews*, *Children's Literature Comprehensive Database*, online, 11 March 2005.
3. Ilene Cooper, rev. of *The Fire-Eaters*, by David Almond, *Booklist* 100.14 (2004), *Children's Literature Reviews*, *Children's Literature Comprehensive Database*, online, 11 March 2005.
4. Debra Nelson, rev. of *The Fire-Eaters*, by David Almond, *Children's Literature* 2004, *Children's Literature Reviews*, *Children's Literature Comprehensive Database*, online, 11 March 2005.
5. Rev. of *The Fire-Eaters*, by David Almond, *Horn Book Guide* 15.2 (2004), *Children's Literature Reviews*, *Children's Literature Comprehensive Database*, online, 11 March 2005.
6. Rev. of *The Fire-Eaters*, by David Almond, *Kirkus Reviews* 72.7 (2004), *Children's Literature Reviews*, *Children's Literature Comprehensive Database*, online, 11 March 2005.
7. Nicolette Jones, rev. of *The Fire-Eaters*, by David Almond, *The Sunday Times* [London] 10 August 2003, *NewsBank*, online, 1 September 2005; Amanda Craig, "Dark with Passion," rev. of *The Fire-Eaters*, by David Almond, *The Times* [London] 3 September 2003, *NewsBank*, online, 1 September 2005.
8. See Sharon Salluzzo, rev. of *The Fire-Eaters*, by David Almond, *Children's Literature* 2004, *Children's Literature Reviews*, *Children's Literature Comprehensive Database*, online, 11 March 2005; and Nicholas Tucker, "Growing Pains in a World on the Brink," rev. of *The Fire-Eaters*, by David Almond, *The Independent* [London] 15 September 2003, *NewsBank*, online, 1 September 2005.

9. Teri S. Lesesne, rev. of *The Fire-Eaters*, by David Almond, *VOYA* 27.4 (2004), *Children's Literature Reviews*, *Children's Literature Comprehensive Database*, online, 11 March 2005.

10. Timnah Card, rev. of *The Fire-Eaters*, by David Almond, *Bulletin of the Center for Children's Books* 57.9 (2004), *Children's Literature Reviews*, *Children's Literature Comprehensive Database*, online, 11 March 2005.

11. Jan Mark, "When the World Held Its Breath," rev. of *The Fire-Eaters*, by David Almond, *The Guardian* [London] 27 September 2003, *Guardian Unlimited*, online, 26 August 2005, http://books.guardian.co.uk/review/story/0,,1049745,00.html.

12. Almond explained in his Boston Globe–Horn Book Award acceptance speech that this northern dialect is called "Geordie," and that it is somewhat characteristic of his own way of speaking. See Almond, "Fiction and Poetry Award Winner," 31–32.

13. Almond, "Fiction and Poetry Award Winner," 35.

14. Several reviewers identify Bobby as being twelve years old. Almond has said that he is eleven. See Almond, "Fiction and Poetry Award Winner," 35.

15. Roberta Seelinger Trites, *Disturbing the Universe: Power and Repression in Adolescent Literature* (Iowa City, IA: University of Iowa Press, 2000) 31.

16. Trites, *Disturbing the Universe*, 123.

17. Trites, *Disturbing the Universe*, 125.

18. Guy Fawkes Night is celebrated on November 5 with the lighting of bonfires. The height of the Cuban Missile Crisis, the day the U2 spy plane was shot down over Cuba, was October 27, 1962. This is the date of the beach scene in the novel. Guy Fawkes Night is thus being celebrated early, in fear and anticipation that the world will end at any minute.

19. Almond, "Fiction and Poetry Award Winner," 36.

CHAPTER EIGHT

~

Gods and Monsters: *Clay*

There is a scene in *Clay*[1] in which the protagonist takes the monster that he and another boy have created out of clay on a guided tour of his hometown. In this scene, which occurs late in the novel and constitutes two entire chapters, the protagonist shows the monster such places as Chilside Road, his grandfather's allotment, St. Elizabeth's Hospital, Dragone's Coffee Shop, St. Patrick's Church, and the cemetery. It is as if, in this scene, Almond is recapitulating places and themes that he introduced in *Counting Stars* and has elaborated in subsequent works. *Clay*, like *The Fire-Eaters*, is set in 1960s Felling, the time and place of Almond's own adolescence, and the adolescent first-person narrator is even named "Davie." Yet, while exploring familiar themes, Almond adds a new twist to those themes. He once again makes use of Gothic motifs, for example, as he did in *Kit's Wilderness* and *Heaven Eyes*, but, unlike in those works, in *Clay* he creates an irredeemably evil character. As in most of his novels, he once again employs magical realism, but this time he gives the magic a sinister, destructive edge. Once again, he demonstrates a fascination with artistic endeavor, but, whereas in previous works he depicted the generative, restorative power of the creative imagination, in *Clay* he explores the dark side of the creative process.

Davie's story is really the story of his relationship with Stephen Rose, a new boy in town who is a couple of years older than Davie. Before

Stephen arrives in Felling, Davie's life is pretty much that of the typical adolescent boy in northern England in the 1960s: he spends his days with his friend Geordie, serving at the altar at St. Patrick's Church, hanging out in the cave at Braddock's Garden, smoking cigarettes stolen from Geordie's dad, battling with a local group of Protestant boys, and lusting after Geordie's older sister—from a safe distance, of course. The biggest conflict in Davie's life is with Martin Mould, an older boy, part of the Protestant gang, who is already on his way to becoming an alcoholic and a delinquent. Into Davie's rather ordinary world comes Stephen Rose, a boy with a mysterious past who has been dismissed from the school where he had been sent to become a priest. With his father dead and his mother in an institution, he has come to live with his aunt, an eccentric but devout woman known as "Crazy Mary." It soon becomes apparent that the boy is an artist, able to create amazingly lifelike clay sculptures, but it also is rumored that he was expelled from school because he was engaging in Satanic rituals and practicing black magic. Stephen, who as it turns out is an adept hypnotist, takes a liking to Davie and in effect seduces him into becoming his accomplice. Together the two boys create a man of clay and then, apparently, bring him to life. When the bully Mouldy is found dead at the bottom of the quarry, Davie assumes that the clay "monster," whom he has named "Clay," is responsible. Later, however, he learns that Stephen himself caused Mouldy's death. Soon thereafter Stephen disappears and is not heard from again. Davie confesses his guilt (by association) to his girlfriend, Maria, and slowly begins to recover from the dark and astonishing events in which he has participated.

Monstrous Transformations

The animation of clay is a trope that Almond introduced in *Heaven Eyes*, where the nearly autistic boy Wilson Cairns possesses the power to animate the small figures that he makes. The idea is extended further in the image of the children being dug out of the mud of the Black Middens and in that of the saint, who is also dug out of the mud, returning to life just in order to escort Grampa's soul to the river. In *Clay* Almond places this trope at the center of the novel and conveys his theme through intertextual allusions to the Jewish myth of the Golem, which Almond has acknowledged as being a major influence on his novel,[2] as well as the most famous work inspired by this myth, Mary Shelley's *Frankenstein*. According to Jewish mythology, the Golem was a creature made of clay, brought to life through magic, whose purpose was to serve and protect its master.[3] The Golem myth has appeared in numerous stories, the most famous of which is the story of "Rabbi Loeb and the Golem of Prague."[4] There are striking parallels between this story, which supposedly took place in 1580,[5] and the events of Almond's novel. Both stories involve the fashioning of a large man out of clay whose purpose is primarily to provide protection from a specific physical threat. Rabbi Loeb created the Golem after hearing that a powerful priest in Prague was planning to accuse the Jews of the city of a new "ritual murder." The Golem was intended to offer protection against the violence that was sure to come.[6] Similarly, Stephen decides to build a clay monster after he learns that Davie and Geordie have been threatened by Mouldy. And, as in the Golem of Prague story, the impetus for the persecution is, at least partly, religious. Davie and Geordie are Catholic while Mouldy and his gang are Protestants. Both the myth and Almond's novel involve elaborate rituals by which the clay figure is brought to life. Rabbi Loeb was assisted by his son-in-law and his pupil, and, before they began the ritual of bringing the creature to life, they undertook a rite of purification. In order to animate the creature, they placed in its mouth a piece of parchment on which had been written the true name of God.[7] In *Clay* Stephen is assisted by Davie, and they wear white shifts, while conducting the ritual in a cave illuminated by candles. The key to animating the lifeless lump, according to Stephen, is to place a bit of the communion elements into the creature's body. Ultimately, in both stories, the creature is returned to a lifeless mass because he is no longer needed and is considered potentially dangerous.[8]

Clay also recalls *Frankenstein* in its concern with animating (or reanimating) a lifeless mass, and, in fact, one night Davie and his parents see the old black-and-white movie on television. Shelley's novel focuses on one man's perversion of science in his quest to become equal to God, and Almond has said that one of his concerns in writing *Clay* was the ethical issues surrounding cloning.[9] At one point Davie tells his girlfriend Maria that one day humans may be able to create life in test tubes, to which she replies, "'Trouble with that is . . . mebbe we won't know where to stop'" (115). Admittedly, no scientific explanation is offered for Stephen's and Davie's powers—if, in fact, they really do bring the creature to life. However, the white smocks they wear when performing the ritual suggest the white lab coats of scientists, the high priests of modern civilization. A victim of his own hubris, Victor Frankenstein, the prototypical mad scientist, is destroyed by the monster he has created. Stephen is not destroyed but rather disappears, while Davie "deactivates" the monster. In both Shelley's and Almond's novels, the creatures, while certainly destructive, seem more sinned against than sinning, having been thrust into a world in which they are doomed to be eternal outcasts. Both works suggest that the real monstrosity lies not in the unfortunate creatures, but in their monomaniacal creators. The theme of science and technology gone awry is further emphasized, albeit in a more subtle way, by the context of the novel—both that of its setting and that of its creation. Set in the early 1960s, *Clay* recalls the setting of *The Fire-Eaters*, in which the specters of the Cuban Missile Crisis and nuclear destruction figure prominently. Although the bomb in not really an issue in *Clay*, surely it is not too much of a stretch to equate the monster, who is created for the purposes of protection and revenge, with nuclear weapons, which were developed for similar reasons. Moreover, the novel was written during the war in Iraq and its aftermath and the proliferation of terrorist attacks, and Almond has acknowledged the influence of that conflict on both *The Fire-Eaters* and *Clay*.[10] The skirmishes between the two groups of boys in *Clay* remind us of the war games in *The Fire-Eaters* and reflect, in miniature, the "real" wars fought by boys (and now girls) not much older than the characters of the novel. Davie and Geordie refer to their fights with the other boys, which are due largely to religious differences, as "battles." The monster, then, may be seen as a symbol of war machinery in general.

The Dark Side of Magic

A key question that the novel does not resolve is whether Stephen and Davie actually bring the clay figure to life, or whether Davie's perception that this is the case is actually a product of Stephen's hypnotic powers. Stephen is adept at hypnosis, a skill he apparently learned from his grandfather Rose. He regularly puts his aunt Mary into a trance so that he can be free from her possible interference with his work, although it is unclear exactly what it is about his sculpting he thinks she might object to. On several different occasions when Davie is watching Stephen try to animate his clay figures, Davie notes that Stephen passes his hand in front of his eyes—the same gesture Davie sees him use to put Mary into a trance. The implication is that Stephen may be using hypnosis to make Davie think he sees the clay figures move, when, in fact, it is just a mind's trick. Later, after the boys have supposedly animated the monster they have built, Davie sees the monster lurking at various places—outside his bedroom window, across the schoolyard. No one else, apparently, sees the monster, although Mary says at one point that she "dreamed" she saw a monster. Again, all of this may be a trick of the mind, the effect of Stephen's hypnotic skill. But, then again, maybe not. The novel leaves open the possibility that indeed Stephen and Davie are able to bring the monster to life, and ultimately to return it to the dust. In other words, the novel does not foreclose the possibility of "real" magic.

Stephen Rose is a character type we have seen before in Almond's work. As a troubled orphan, he reminds us of the Whitegates children in *Heaven Eyes*, particularly the wounded and cynical January Carr. As a shadow figure, a dark character to whom the main character feels a strong, inexplicable attraction, he recalls Askew in *Kit's Wilderness*. Like Kit with Askew, Davie is horrified by Stephen but at the same time he recognizes that "something had drawn us together, that somehow we were meant to be together" (166). But, unlike January and Askew, Stephen experiences no catharsis and no redemption. Rather than being helped by his association with Davie, as Father O'Mahoney hoped he would be, Stephen instead nearly destroys Davie. After the boy disappears, Davie imagines that every murder and every maiming he hears about must be the work of Stephen Rose. Davie sees him in his dreams and thinks he sees him among the crowds in town. He is convinced that one day Stephen will return, and he finds himself hoping, much to his horror, that Stephen is dead.

And therein lies an important theme of the novel: if Stephen seems irredeemably evil, in some ways he also reflects a part of Davie's psyche.

Having once been attacked by Mouldy, there is a part of Davie that believes the world would be better off if people like Mouldy were not in it. Nor is Davie alone in his feelings. Geordie, too, would like to see Mouldy gone, and he is clearly relieved, even pleased, when Mouldy is found dead at the bottom of the quarry. Whoever or whatever else Stephen Rose may be, for both Davie and Geordie he also represents their own dark desires, things they think about doing but would never do on their own. In that sense, Stephen can be seen as the embodiment of Freud's notion of the unbridled Id, the seat of amoral, unconscious drives. He claims that God has abandoned humankind, that he "nicked off" sometime around 1945 and the end of World War II. There is no god for Stephen to be beholden to. He, therefore, becomes his own god, using his powers for destructive purposes. Davie too has serious doubts about God's involvement in human affairs, and yet he continues to attend church, go to confession, and invest belief in the power of the communion elements. In spite of his occasional agnostic statements, Davie does not quite have the courage of his lack of conviction, and he easily accepts Stephen's story about his angelic vision on the beach at Whitley Bay, a story Stephen later admits is completely fabricated. In many ways, it is tempting to see Davie as the innocent, corrupted by the wily ways of Stephen Rose. But the truth is more complex. Yes, Davie is more naïve than Stephen, but, as his thoughts demonstrate, he too harbors dark, destructive desires. Clearly, then, Stephen is not the only monster in the novel. To Davie and Geordie, Mouldy is the monster. Geordie calls him a monster, and Davie, in thinking about the gang of Protestant boys with whom they are battling, reflects that "Mouldy was the only really evil one" (22). But in wanting Mouldy dead, Davie and Geordie reveal their own potential for monstrosity.

Stephen and Davie's associations with religion bear closer examination, for it reflects Almond's own tumultuous relationship to his Catholic upbringing. Stephen, apparently, believes in nothing except his own invincibility. For him, religion is a means to his own selfish ends. His attraction to the priesthood—and this, apparently, was genuine enough—stemmed from his desire to become more than human. He clearly assumed at an early age that the priests were consorts of the devil, privy to the secrets of black magic. At the school for boys interested in the priesthood, it was Stephen who proved to be the devil's consort, leading other boys down the path of destruction. One boy, it is said, went insane. To be sure, these reports come from Stephen himself, and how much he is posturing in talking to Davie is unclear. However, one thing seems certain: Stephen was dismissed from the school for highly objectionable behavior, either practicing black magic or at least claiming that he did. Stephen's use of religion is a perversion of the Church's teachings, and his greatest sin—and that would seem not to be too strong a word within the context of the novel—is in trying to assume the role of God as creator.

Davie's association with religion is both less intense and less perverse than Stephen's. Davie not only attends church, but he and his friend Geordie regularly serve at the altar. At the same time, they mock their "piety" by laughing about how holy they feel after confession, even while they continue to do the very things they have just confessed. Davie even goes so far as to admit to Geordie that he is not sure he really believes in God and religion anymore. Ironically, it is through his relationship with Stephen that Davie betrays the persistence of his perhaps subconscious belief. He obviously believes Stephen's story about his angelic vision, and when Stephen asks him to steal a bit of the Body and Blood from communion, he does so willingly, thinking that the elements have the power to animate the clay monster the two boys have created. Later, when Davie learns that Stephen has lied to him, he is shaken—and forced to acknowledge his prior belief in the supernatural. In many ways, Davie's experience with religion parallels that of *his* creator, David Almond, in that the adolescent Almond also struggled with his religious beliefs, finally rejecting organized religion but never letting go of the Church's rich imagery and powerful stories. These, in fact, are elements that continue to infuse his own writings, as is strongly evident in *Clay*.

Catholicism Revisited

As noted in the previous chapter, *The Fire-Eaters* is Almond's most critical portrait of priests and the Church, as embodied in his portrayal of the sadistic tyrant Mr. Todd. Not since the stories of *Counting Stars* had Almond been so overtly negative in his portrayal of religious institutions. *Clay*, by contrast, offers a much more sympathetic portrait of priests and religion, and the one truly evil character here is clearly aligned against the Church. Father O'Mahoney, the priest of St. Patrick's, is a kind, gentle person who seems to understand the trials of adolescence and responds by being supportive rather than judgmental. When he realizes that Davie and Geordie are more concerned with the "tips" they get from serving at weddings and funerals, the father, rather than rebuking the boys, simply chuckles softly. For his own part, he seems to enjoy the simple pleasures of life, reflecting at one point on what a lovely day it would be for a game of golf. He is perhaps the primary reason Davie continues to go to confession: Father O'Mahoney is someone Davie feels comfortable talking to. When, after having lost his parents, Stephen comes to live with his aunt in Felling, it is Father O'Mahoney who looks out for the boy, who asks Stephen to make clay figurines of the apostles, and encourages Davie and Geordie to befriend him. Rather than judging Stephen, Father O'Mahoney tries to steer him through a very difficult time. In short, Father O'Mahoney proves to be both human and humane: unsanctimonious and unpretentious, he is the epitome of a good man.

Father O'Mahoney's greatest flaw, at least in Davie's eyes and certainly in Stephen's, is that he is perhaps a bit *too* human, to the point of being ineffectual. For one thing, he seems unaware of what is really going on around him. He does not know, for example, that Davie has stolen bits of the Body and Blood of Christ during communion. Nor does he realize that Stephen has utter contempt for him. It is clear from his interactions with Davie during confession that he believes that by labeling sin, one can ultimately overcome it. He therefore seems eager to identify the exact violations exemplified by Davie's various behaviors: theft, blasphemy, and lack of charity. But these "sins" are fairly minor ones: stealing a cigarette, drinking altar wine, calling someone a name. It is significant that Davie never confesses to Father O'Mahoney the sin that disturbs him the most, i. e., helping Stephen create the monster who, Davie believes, is partly responsible for Mouldy's death. He confesses instead to his girlfriend, Maria. Stephen is more blunt in his assessment of Father O'Mahoney when he says, "'Damn him! . . . Damn his bliddy ordinariness'" (91). The word "ordinariness" is significant, suggesting that Stephen's main objection to the priest is that he displays none of the supernatural power that Stephen finds so compelling. It is not surprising then that the priest, in spite of his good intentions, is not able to help the boy. When Davie admonishes Father O'Mahoney for failing to look out for Stephen, the priest makes his own confession, acknowledging his own ineffectuality. He believes, however, that there is still hope for Stephen's return and redemption. Ironically, he sees Stephen as a troubled but otherwise "'ordinary boy'" (284), reflecting in his (mis)perception the very trait that Stephen abhorred in him. Father O'Mahoney believes that humans are often victims of their own weakness, but that evil is "'very rare,'" just as true goodness is rare (283). As Almond portrays him, the priest is clearly a good man, but it is unclear whether we should admire his wisdom or deplore his naiveté. Like the ultimate fate of Stephen Rose, that question is left unresolved.

The person to whom Davie is finally able to confess his dark secret is his girlfriend, Maria O'Callaghan, whose name echoes that of the Virgin Mary, the Mother of Christ. In Roman Catholic teaching, Mary is not only the Mother of God but also a co-participant in the redemption of humankind.[11] In a significant way, Maria proves to be Davie's salvation from the psychological damage incurred by his association with Stephen. By everyone's account, Maria, like her namesake, is a young woman of transcendent beauty. She is the one who seeks out Davie, sending a message through their mutual friend Frances Malone that she "fancies" him. Moreover, she continues to be interested in him even when he shuns her and when she sees Stephen kiss Davie on the cheek. Most importantly, she serves as Davie's confessor, believing him when he tells her about the monster he and Stephen created. She is supportive, not judgmental, and she assures Davie that he is not mad. Taking two pieces of clay from the remnants of the monster, she fashions two figures, one of Davie and one of herself—and then she continues to make clay figures of many of the people in their community, including their parents, Geordie, Frances, Crazy Mary, and Father O'Mahoney. Maria's action illustrates both her generative and redemptive power, as is suggested by Davie's father's comment when he sees the group of figures: "'It's a congregation of the saints!'" (291). Maria does not seem to be a particularly religious person, although, like most of the youth of Felling, she attends church regularly. Instead, her grace seems natural, suggesting an innate wisdom beyond her years.

There is another Mary in the book as well—Stephen's aunt, whom they call "Crazy Mary.'" So called because, as Davie's mother says, she is "'a devout and troubled soul'" (8), it falls to Mary to look after Stephen after his father dies and his mother is committed to a sanitarium. Somewhat like Father O'Mahoney, Mary fails to see her nephew's true nature, and she is easily duped by him. On more than one occasion, Davie sees Stephen put his aunt into a hypnotic state. It is clear from his actions that Stephen has almost as much contempt for his aunt's piety as he does for Father O'Mahoney's goodness. As a "troubled soul," Mary recalls the Mary Magdalene of the Bible, whose demonic possession was healed by Christ.[12] In her devoutness, she recalls another Mary of the Bible, the mystic Mary of Bethany, who is remembered for anointing Christ's feet with oil in recognition of both his divinity and his impending death.[13] Indeed, Davie's mother says that Mary could be called "'Holy Mary,'" for she is reputed to have "'saints in [her] past'" (8). This saintly lineage, along with the holy water she keeps inside her doorway and the bread and jam she always has available for Stephen and his friends, connects her with the mysticism as well as the anointing and nurturing functions of Mary of Bethany. Stephen's disappearance plunges Mary into despair and causes her to forget how to pray. But Davie helps to restore her soul by presenting her with the locket containing the fragments of the Body and Blood that he originally stole from the altar and that he has reclaimed from the body of the now defunct monster. This locket proves to be a catalyst for Mary, inspiring a vision in which she sees Heaven open up and angels descending to her. Unlike her nephew's angelic vision, Mary's is real—at least to her—and afterwards she is filled with hope for Stephen's return. If Stephen has a chance for salvation, one suspects that it lies in the prayers and devotion of his aunt.

The two Marys in the novel serve similar functions: Maria maintains hope for Davie and does ultimately effect his redemption, while the restoration of Mary's hope for Stephen has the potential at least to effect his redemption. The common thread between the two women is their capacity for belief. Mary's faith and spirituality are more tradition bound and function clearly within the parameters of organized religion. She believes devoutly in God and the teachings of the Catholic Church. By way of comparison, Maria's spirituality seems more natural, her faith in Davie more intuitive. But both reflect a kind of mystical connection to the spiritual realm that we have seen in other Almond characters, such as the "Wild Girl" Elaine, the child called Heaven Eyes, Joe Maloney and his friend Corinna, and Ailsa Spink.

Another View of the Artist

As in a number of Almond's works, an important motif in the novel is the creative process, but in *Clay* he explores the darker side of artistic creation. Generally speaking, in his previous works Almond portrays art as redemptive and artists as admirable. In the "Afterword" to *Wild Girl, Wild Boy*, for example, he describes Elaine as "a bold creative spirit" who is "brave enough to outface [death]."[14] In *Kit's Wilderness*, Askew is saved through his own artistic endeavors (sketching) as well as Kit's (storytelling). And in *Heaven Eyes* Wilson Cairns creates clay figures as a way of "re-creat[ing] some of the childhood he had lost."[15] In *The Fire-Eaters* art serves a more utilitarian purpose, with Daniel's photography exposing the true nature of the tyrannical Mr. Todd. But in *Clay* Almond shows that the creative process is not necessarily redemptive and, in fact, can be used for sinister purposes. He has said that one of his interests in writing the book was to explore the notion of whether the creative process is a force for good or a force for evil.[16] Whereas in his previous works he has suggested that it is a force for good, in this novel it is a force for evil, at least through much of the novel. Stephen Rose, by all accounts, is a very talented artist. Father O'Mahoney clearly assumes that engaging in the creative process can have a healing effect on the boy, for soon after Stephen comes to Felling, the priest asks him to make figures of the apostles for the school. Stephen initially tries to fulfill his task by carving pieces of wood and working with clay he has found nearby, but to no avail: he thinks the results are "'crap'" (32). He says that he needs the right kind of clay, something akin to the primordial muck out of which life originally emerged, so that he can create something out of "'nowt,'" as he says, "'Like God did'" (33). Davie and Geordie know that the pond in a nearby cave will provide Stephen with the kind of clay he needs, and in showing him this pond they become implicated in his work. The figures that Stephen then makes are magnificent. As Prat Parker, the art teacher, says, they are "'astonishing,'" remarkably life-like yet with "'an inner grace, an inner . . . light'" (49; ellipsis in original). Stephen's great talent, it turns out, is to create amazingly life-like figures—and, even more amazing, to actually bring them to life. Whether Stephen actually is able to invest his figures with life, he clearly is able to produce that impression on Davie (perhaps through hypnotism). More than once, Stephen describes himself as like God, referring to his ability to create something out of nothing, just as God created humankind out of the dust of the earth. As an artist, he does seem to have God-like powers, but he uses his powers for destructive rather than benevolent purposes. Moreover, Stephen uses his artistic skills and his powers as a hypnotist to manipulate others' perceptions for his own dark purposes and in so doing is guilty of what Hawthorne described as the violation of the human soul. And this is Stephen's great flaw. When Davie asks Prat if "'an artist is a kind of God,'" Prat replies that equating human creativity with divine creativity "'has led many down a darkening and ever more terrifying path'" (96–97). An artist, according to Prat, is ultimately "'simply human'" but with a God-given talent (97). Stephen ultimately cannot accept his own humanity, his own limitations.

And it is Stephen's monomaniacal striving to be like God that turns him into a monster. When Geordie fashions a monster out of clay in art class, Prat says that "'what the artist does is give an outer form to his inner self'" (96). This appears to be the case with Stephen when he creates scores of goblins and unfinished things and places them in the niches of the wall in the cave. And it is certainly the case when he, with Davie's help, fashions the monster out of clay and then brings it to life. The monster is created to destroy Mouldy, but, as it turns out, Stephen is the one who pushes Mouldy over the edge of the quarry, sending him to his death. It is Stephen who is the true monster. In his striving to be like God, he has become a monster. In his thoughts and actions, Stephen exemplifies the dangerous aspect of the creative process: as Prat says, "'[the human] passion to create goes hand in hand with our passion to destroy'" (212).

The clay monster comes to symbolize both aspects of the creative process. It is not the monster who pushes Mouldy over the edge of the quarry. As Stephen tells Davie, the monster ultimately could not kill because he "'had too much of the Davie in [him]'" (233). Had he been solely Stephen's creation, the monster would not have hesitated to carry out Stephen's command. The implication is that Davie, while exhibiting the potential for the kind of evil actions that Stephen commits, ultimately has more good in him than Stephen. The monster, then, is neither destructive nor constructive. Before it has a chance to do anything, it is returned to a lifeless lump of clay. However, Maria uses the remains of the monster for constructive purposes, creating a multitude of clay figures that represent a "congregation of the saints." Davie too transforms his experience with Stephen and the monster into art, specifically the story we have been reading. At the end of the novel, he says that he has tried to speak the tale many times but has always been stifled by "the craziness" (295) in the story. As a result, he has now written it down, offering to us his ultimate confession, the realization that "crazy things can be the truest things of all" (296). And, to push the analogy a bit further, it seems fair to suggest that in writing the novel Almond has fashioned his own work of art from previous tales, specifically "The Golem of Prague" and *Frankenstein*. If *Clay* suggests that the creative process has a dark, potentially destructive side, then it also shows that artistic creation also has the potential to be infinitely regenerative and ultimately redemptive.

Notes

1. As this book went to press, *Clay* was due to be published by Hodder Children's Books in the United Kingdom in November 2005. My discussion of the book is based on the bound proof graciously made available to me by David Almond and Hodder Children's Books.
2. David Almond, personal interview, 21 April 2005.
3. Micha F. Lindemans, "Golem," *Encyclopedia Mythica*, online, 2 August 2005 http://www.pantheon.org/mythica.html.
4. Ilil Arbel, "Rabbi Loeb," *Encyclopedia Mythica*, online, 2 August 2005 http://www.pantheon.org/mythica.html.
5. Arbel, "Rabbi Loeb."
6. Arbel, "Rabbi Loeb."
7. Arbel, "Rabbi Loeb."
8. Arbel, "Rabbi Loeb."
9. Almond, personal interview.
10. Almond, personal interview.

11. Jaroslav Jan Pelikan, "Mary," *Encyclopedia Britannica Online*, online, 4 August 2005.

12. J. E. Fallon, "Mary Magdalene, St.," *New Catholic Encyclopedia*, 2nd. (Detroit: Gale, 2003).

13. Fallon, "Mary Magdalene, St."

14. David Almond, "Afterword," *Wild Girl, Wild Boy: A Play* (London: Hodder Children's Books, 2002) 86.

15. David Almond, *Heaven Eyes* (New York: Delacorte, 2001) 29.

16. Almond, personal interview.

CHAPTER NINE

~

Afterword: Magical Realism Revisited

The capacity of young people to recognize the presence of the magical amid the realities of everyday life is, as we have seen, a predominant theme of all of Almond's works. Though he does not consider himself to be a particularly religious person, he acknowledges that a religious impulse is reflected in his work.[1] Indeed most of his adolescent characters, if not religious exactly, are profoundly spiritual, and, moreover, their spirituality is closely associated with the creative impulse. Almond has said that, if there is a God, he is "a very generous God," who has placed "a creative spark" within each of us.[2]

And herein lies the crux of the matter for Almond's use of magical realism. One's ability to see the magic in the world derives from that ability to recognize and respond to the workings of the creative imagination. Almond's novels are filled with adolescents engaged in creative endeavors like drawing, sculpting, acting, photography, acrobatics, and, especially, writing stories. These activities, and the young people who practice them, attest to the power of the creative imagination in helping the adolescent to make sense of life, forge an identity, and retain that magical sensibility into adulthood. In his acceptance speech for the Michael L. Printz Award, Almond spoke particularly of the power of narrative: " . . . the mysterious circuits of the human brain, no matter what its age, will always be set to spark by narrative and language."[3]

Elsewhere he has written that it is "stories that help to keep the world alive."[4] Here, then, is the connection between memory and magic: the transformative power of narrative helps to connect us to one another and to reveal the magic within the world and within ourselves. Stories, Almond explains, "bring us together because each of us has that thing that is both ordinary and quite astonishing: the imagination, which allows the writer and the reader, the teller and the listener to reach out to each other."[5]

Almond's own narratives have followed a trajectory from the (mostly) straight realism of the transitional work *Counting Stars* to the more overt magical realism of *Skellig*, *Kit's Wilderness*, *Heaven Eyes*, and *Secret Heart*. *The Fire-Eaters* represents a return to a more realistic, less magical mode of writing. Almond himself has described the novel as a "deliberate turning back from so much magic."[6] *Clay*, on the other hand, signals a return to magical realism, but in this book the magic has dark overtones. Overall, it seems that his works are getting darker and are incorporating more social criticism. He has acknowledged the effects of the Iraq War and terrorism on his ruminations about the nature of evil in both *The Fire-Eaters* and *Clay*. As Maggie Ann Bowers points out, magical realism has proven to be a viable mode for writers engaged in criticism of the dominant culture.[7] Whether it will continue to be a viable mode for Almond in his evolution as a writer and social critic remains to be seen. But one suspects that it will, for, to Almond, the fundamental function of literature is to reveal the magical among the mundane. In an article for *The Times*, he has written,

> Ordinary kids live ordinary lives in ordinary places, and always ordinariness is just a front. If there are demons, this is the world in which they might pester us. If there are miracles, this is where they might take place.[8]

What does the future hold for Almond? He says that he sees himself primarily as a young adult novelist, but that he also enjoys working in other formats, drama and picture books especially. In some ways, the three main characters of *Kit's Wilderness* embody Almond's own artistic interests. Allie Keenan is the consummate actor, who loves to re-create herself each time she performs. Almond admits that, while he approached the writing of his first play, *Wild Girl, Wild Boy*, with a bit of trepidation, he soon realized that he "just loved it; it was fantastic."[9] Since then, he has adapted *Skellig* and *Heaven Eyes* for the stage, as well as some of the family stories in *Counting Stars*.[10] In the process, he has discovered that something about the way he writes fiction translates well to the stage. He has even written the libretto for an operatic version of *Skellig*, with American composer Todd Makover, and there are film versions of *Skellig* and *The Fire-Eaters* in the works.[11] Like the storyteller Kit Watson working with the sketch artist John Askew, Almond has also found the opportunity to collaborate with illustrators on children's picture books to be very rewarding. In fact, he enjoyed the experience of writing *Kate, the Cat and the Moon* so much that he has now written a second picture book.[12] But, like Kit, Almond sees himself primarily as a prose writer, and he expects to continue writing young adult novels for some time to come. He has said that his next novel will be "a different kind of realism," one influenced by his writing of picture books and plays.[13] As he evolves as a writer, Almond is clearly experiencing a kind of intertexuality within his own works, with novels becoming plays becoming films becoming operas apparently as easily as Joe Maloney becomes a tiger or Kate becomes a cat.

Almond appears to be at the height of his creative powers. This book then is not intended to be—indeed *cannot* be—a definitive study of Almond's career. Instead, it is offered as an introduction to the remarkable work of a man considered by many to be among the best authors writing for young people today. No doubt, Almond will continue to produce award-winning literary works, and an updated version of this book will be required in a few years. An image that he has returned to again and again in speeches and interviews is that of himself as an adolescent boy, sitting in a small branch library in Felling-upon-Tyne and dreaming that one day he would see his name on the covers of the books. Now that there are books in libraries with his name on them, his hope, he has said, is for young people to read his books and to be "infect[ed] with their own dream, that one day they'll walk into the library, reach up to a shelf, and see a book not with David Almond's name but with their own name printed on the cover."[14] In the meantime, devoted readers can look forward to seeing many more books with

Almond's name on the covers, books filled with memory and magic, books that will inspire young people to dream their own dreams.

Notes

1. David Almond, personal interview, 21 April 2005.

2. David Almond, Interview with Bel Mooney, *Devout Sceptics*, BBC, London, 8 July 2004, online, 11 May 2005, www.bbc.co.uk/religion/programmes/devout_sceptics/index.html.

3. David Almond, "The 2001 Michael L. Printz Award Acceptance Speech," *Journal of Youth Services in Libraries* 14.4 (2001): 15, *WilsonSelectPlus*, online, 13 February 2003.

4. David Almond, "Afterword," *Wild Girl, Wild Boy: A Play* (London: Hodder Books, 2002) 87.

5. David Almond, "Fiction and Poetry Award Winner," *The Horn Book* 81.1 (2005): 36.

6. Almond, personal interview.

7. Maggie Ann Bowers, *Magic(al) Realism* (New York: Routledge, 2004) 69.

8. David Almond, "Magic All Around If You Only Know How to Look," *The Times* [London] 6 August 2003, *NewsBank*, online, 1 September 2005.

9. Almond, personal interview.

10. Almond, personal interview. *Heaven Eyes* is scheduled to premiere at the Edinburgh Fringe Festival in August 2005.

11. Almond, personal interview.

12. Almond, personal interview. As of this writing, Almond is looking for an illustrator for his second picture book.

13. Almond, personal interview.

14. David Almond, "The 2001 Michael L. Printz Award Acceptance Speech."

~

Bibliography

Primary Sources

Collections of Short Stories

Almond, David. *Counting Stars.* London: Hodder Books, 2000. New York: Delacorte P, 2002.

———. *A Kind of Heaven.* North Shields, Northumberland, UK: Iron Press, 1997.

———. *Sleepless Nights.* North Shields, Northumberland, UK: Iron Press, 1985.

Essays

Almond, David. "Give Our Kids a Break." *The Sunday Times* [London] 3 October 1999. *NewsBank.* Online. 1 September 2005.

———. "Magic All Around If You Only Know How to Look." *The Times* [London] 6 August 2003. *NewsBank.* Online. 1 September 2005.

Novels

Almond, David. *The Fire-Eaters.* London: Hodder Children's Books, 2003. New York: Delacorte Press, 2004.

———. *Heaven Eyes.* London: Hodder Children's Books, 2000. New York: Delacorte Press, 2001.

———. *Kit's Wilderness.* London: Hodder Children's Books, 1999. New York: Delacorte Press, 2000.

———. *Secret Heart*. London: Hodder Children's Books, 2001. New York: Delacorte Press, 2002.

———. *Skellig*. London: Hodder Children's Books, 1998. New York: Delacorte Press, 1999.

Picture Book

Almond, David, and Stephen Lambert, illus. *Kate, the Cat and the Moon*. London: Hodder Children's Books, 2004.

Plays

Almond, David. *Skellig: The Play*. London: Hodder Children's Books, 2003.

———. *Wild Girl, Wild Boy: A Play*. London: Hodder Children's Books, 2002.

Selected Speeches

Almond, David. "The 2001 Michael L. Printz Award Acceptance Speech." *Journal of Youth Services in Libraries* 14.4 (2001): 12–15, 23. *WilsonSelectPlus*. Online. 13 February 2003.

———. "Fiction and Poetry Award Winner." *Horn Book* 81.1 (2005): 31–36.

Secondary Sources

Articles and Book Chapters

Alberge, Dalya. "Author Brings 'Stifling' School System to Book." *The Times* [London] 15 July 1999. *NewsBank*. Online. 1 September 2005.

Brennan, Geraldine. "The Game Called Death: Frightening Fictions by David Almond, Philip Gross, and Lesley Howarth." *Frightening Fiction: R. L. Stine, Robert Westall, David Almond, and Others*. Ed. Kimberly Reynolds, Geraldine Brennan, and Kevin McCarron. New York: Continuum, 2001. 92–127.

"David Almond." *Contemporary Authors Online*. Gale, 2003. *Literature Resource Center*. Online. 23 January 2004.

Graham, Katherine V. "Still 'Burning Bright': William Blake's Influence on Contemporary Writers for Children." 31st Annual Conference of the Children's Literature Association. Fresno, CA. 10–12 June 2004.

"A Hit from a Myth." *The Observer* [London] 23 November 2003. *Guardian Unlimited*. Online. 1 September 2005, http://observer.guardian.co.uk/review/story/0,6903,1091171,00.html.

Johnston, Rosemary Ross. "Carnivals, the Carnivalesque, *The Magic Puddin'*, and David Almond's *Wild Girl, Wild Boy*: Toward a Theorizing of Children's Plays." *Children's Literature in Education* 34.2 (2003): 131–46.

Latham, Don. "Magical Realism and the Child Reader: The Case of David Almond's *Skellig*." *The Looking Glass: An Online Children's Literature Journal*. 10.1 (2006). Available at www.the-looking-glass.net/.

Mordue, Mark. "The Gentle Dreamer." *Sunday Age* (Melbourne). 1 June 2003: Agenda, 10. *Lexis-Nexis*. Online. 3 June 2003.

Wagner, Erica. "Literature That Knows No Limits." *The Times* (London). 15 July 1999. *Lexis-Nexis*. Online. 4 June 2003.

Ward, David. "Burning Bright." *The Guardian* (London). 17 December 2002: Education, 2. *Lexis-Nexis*. Online. 29 May 2003.

Selected Interviews

Achuka. "Achuka Interview: David Almond." 1999. Online. 11 May 2005, www.achuka.co.uk/archive/interviews/daint.php.

Almond, David. Interview with Bel Mooney. *Devout Sceptics*. BBC. London. 8 July 2004. Online. 11 May 2005, www.bbc.co.uk/religion/programmes/devout_sceptics/index.shtml.

———. Online chat session. *Blast*. BBC. [n.d.] Online. 9 March 2005, www.bbc.co.uk/blast/about/ask/dalmond_transcript.shtml.

———. Personal e-mail. 13 May 2005.

———. Personal interview. 21 April 2005.

Comerford, Lydia Bill. "The British Invasion: *PW* Speaks to Five Authors Who Have Crossed the Atlantic and Found American Readers." *Publishers Weekly* 249.26 (2002): 26. *Literature Resource Center*. Online. 11 May 2005.

Cooper, Ilene. "The *Booklist* Interview." *Booklist* 96 (2000): 898. *Literature Resource Center*. Online. 4 June 2003.

———. "The *Booklist* Interview." *Booklist* 97 (2001): 1464. *Literature Resource Center*. Online. 11 May 2005.

Devereaux, Elizabeth. "Flying Starts." *Publishers Weekly* 26 (28 June 1999): 25. *Literature Resource Center*. Online. 29 May 2003.

Maughan, Shannon. "David Almond: Interview." Teenreads.com. 7 April 2000. Online. 11 May 2005, http://teenreads.com/authors/au-almond-david.asp.

Odean, Kathleen. "Mystic Man." *School Library Journal* 47.4 (2001): 48–52. *WilsonSelectPlus*. Online. 1 June 2003.

Pike, Joseph. "David Almond." Jubilee Books. March 2002. Online. 11 May 2005, www.jubileebooks.co.uk/jubilee/magazine/authors/david_almond/interview.asp.

Richards, Linda. "January Interview: David Almond." *January Magazine*. February 2002. Online. 11 May 2005, www.januarymagazine.com/profiles/almond.html.

Ridge, Judith. "An Interview with David Almond: Part One." May 2003. Online. 11 May 2005, www.misrule.com.au/almond1.html.
———. "An Interview with David Almond: Part Two." May 2003. Online. 11 May 2005, www.misrule.com.au/almond2.html.

Selected Reviews

Counting Stars

Bush, Elizabeth. Rev. of *Counting Stars*, by David Almond. *Bulletin of the Center for Children's Books* 55.7 (2002). *Children's Literature Reviews, Children's Literature Comprehensive Database*. Online. 29 May 2003.
Maguire, Gregory. Rev. of *Counting Stars*, by David Almond. *Horn Book* 78.2 (2002): 207–8.
McLoughlin, William. Rev. of *Counting Stars*, by David Almond. *School Library Journal* 48.3 (2002): 225.
Pullman, Philip. "Spellbinding Realism." Rev. of *Counting Stars*, by David Almond. *Guardian Unlimited* 28 September 2000. Online. 1 September 2005, http://books.guardian.co.uk/booksareforever/story/0,,373653,00.html.
Rev. of *Counting Stars*, by David Almond. *Kirkus Reviews* 70.6 (2002). *Children's Literature Reviews, Children's Literature Comprehensive Database*. Online. 29 May 2003.
Rochman, Hazel. Rev. of *Counting Stars*, by David Almond. *Booklist* 98.11 (2002). *Children's Literature Reviews, Children's Literature Comprehensive Database*. Online. 29 May 2003.
Wagner, Erica. "Vivid Bedtime Stories for Young and Old Alike." Rev. of *Counting Stars*, by David Almond. *The Times* [London] 15 November 2000. *Lexis-Nexis*. Online. 4 June 2003.
Williams, Sherrie. Rev. of *Counting Stars*, by David Almond. VOYA 25.3 (2002), *Children's Literature Reviews, Children's Literature Comprehensive Database*. Online. 29 May 2003.

The Fire-Eaters

Card, Timnah. Rev. of *The Fire-Eaters*, by David Almond. *Bulletin of the Center for Children's Books* 57.9 (2004). *Children's Literature Reviews, Children's Literature Comprehensive Database*. Online. 11 March 2005.
Coghlan, Susanna. Rev. of *The Fire-Eaters*, by David Almond. *Inis—The Magazine of Children's Books Ireland* no. 7 (2003). *Children's Literature Reviews, Children's Literature Comprehensive Database*. Online. 11 March 2005.
Cooper, Ilene. Rev. of *The Fire-Eaters*, by David Almond. *Booklist* 100.14 (2004). *Children's Literature Reviews, Children's Literature Comprehensive Database*. Online. 11 March 2005.

Craig, Amanda. "Dark with Passion." Rev. of *The Fire-Eaters*, by David Almond. *The Times* [London] 3 September 2003. *NewsBank*. Online. 1 September 2005.

Jones, Nicolette. Rev. of *The Fire-Eaters*, by David Almond. *The Sunday Times* [London] 10 August 2003. *NewsBank*. Online. 1 September 2005.

Lesesne, Teri S. Rev. of *The Fire-Eaters*, by David Almond. *VOYA* 27.4 (2004). *Children's Literature Reviews, Children's Literature Comprehensive Database*. Online. 11 March 2005.

Mark, Jan. "When the World Held Its Breath." Rev. of *The Fire-Eaters*, by David Almond. *The Guardian* [London] 27 September 2003. *Guardian Unlimited*. Online. 26 August 2005, http://books.guardian.co.uk/review/story/0,,1049745,00.html.

Nelson, Debra. Rev. of *The Fire-Eaters*, by David Almond. *Children's Literature* 2004. *Children's Literature Reviews, Children's Literature Comprehensive Database*. Online. 11 March 2005.

Rev. of *The Fire-Eaters*, by David Almond. *Horn Book Guide* 15.2 (2004). *Children's Literature Reviews, Children's Literature Comprehensive Database*. Online. 11 March 2005.

Rev. of *The Fire-Eaters*, by David Almond. *Kirkus Reviews* 72.7 (2004). *Children's Literature Reviews, Children's Literature Comprehensive Database*. Online. 11 March 2005.

Salluzzo, Sharon. Rev. of *The Fire-Eaters*, by David Almond. *Children's Literature* 2004. *Children's Literature Reviews, Children's Literature Comprehensive Database*. Online. 11 March 2005.

Tucker, Nicholas. "Growing Pains in a World on the Brink." Rev. of *The Fire-Eaters*, by David Almond. *The Independent* [London] 15 September 2003. *NewsBank*. Online. 1 September 2005.

Heaven Eyes

Cooper, Ilene. Rev. of *Heaven Eyes*, by David Almond. *Booklist* 97.9 (2001). *Children's Literature Reviews, Children's Literature Comprehensive Database*. Online. 29 May 2003.

Del Negro, Janice M. Rev. of *Heaven Eyes*, by David Almond. *Bulletin of the Center for Children's Books* 54.8 (2001). *Children's Literature Reviews, Children's Literature Comprehensive Database*. Online. 29 May 2003.

Gardner, Lyn. Rev. of *Heaven Eyes*, by David Almond. *Education Guardian .co.uk* 29 March 2005. *Guardian Unlimited*. Online. 1 September 2005, http://education.guardian.co.uk/childrensbooks/11plus/review/0,,153450,00.html.

Johnson, Sarah. "Touching Tale of an Escape, a Journey and a Magical Child." Rev. of *Heaven Eyes*, by David Almond. *The Times* [London] 20 January 2000. *Lexis-Nexis*. Online. 4 June 2003.

Munat, Florence H. Rev. of *Heaven Eyes*, by David Almond. *VOYA* 24.1 (2001). *Children's Literature Reviews, Children's Literature Comprehensive Database*. Online. 29 May 2003.

Rev. of *Heaven Eyes*, by David Almond. *Horn Book Guide* 12.2 (2001). *Children's Literature Reviews, Children's Literature Comprehensive Database*. Online. 29 May 2003.

Rev. of *Heaven Eyes*, by David Almond. *Kirkus Reviews* 69.4 (2001). *Children's Literature Reviews, Children's Literature Comprehensive Database*. Online. 29 May 2003.

Rohrlick, Paula. Rev. of *Heaven Eyes*, by David Almond. *KLIATT Review* 35.2 (2001). *Children's Literature Reviews, Children's Literature Comprehensive Database*. Online. 29 May 2003.

Salluzzo, Sharon. Rev. of *Heaven Eyes*, by David Almond. *Children's Literature* 2001. *Children's Literature Reviews, Children's Literature Comprehensive Database*. Online. 29 May 2003.

Kate, the Cat and the Moon

Eccleshare, Julia. "Julia Eccleshare's Picture-Book Roundup." Rev. of *Kate, the Cat and the Moon*, by David Almond, illus. Stephen Lambert. *The Guardian* [London] 13 November 2004. *NewsBank*. Online. 1 September 2005.

Jones, Nicolette. Rev. of *Kate, the Cat, and the Moon*, by David Almond, illus. Stephen Lambert. *The Sunday Times* [London] 24 October 2004. *NewsBank*. Online. 1 September 2005.

Kit's Wilderness

Ammon, Bette. Rev. of *Kit's Wilderness*, by David Almond. *VOYA* 23.1 (2000). *Children's Literature Reviews, Children's Literature Comprehensive Database*. Online. 29 May 2003.

Bloom, Susan P. Rev. of *Kit's Wilderness*, by David Almond. *Horn Book* 76.2 (2000): 192.

Bush, Elizabeth. Rev. of *Kit's Wilderness*, by David Almond. *Bulletin of the Center for Children's Books* 53.5 (2000). *Children's Literature Reviews, Children's Literature Comprehensive Database*. Online. 29 May 2003.

Cooper, Ilene. Rev. of *Kit's Wilderness*, by David Almond. *Booklist* 96.9 and 10 (2000). *Children's Literature Reviews, Children's Literature Comprehensive Database*. Online. 29 May 2003.

Donelson, Ken. Rev. of *Kit's Wilderness*, by David Almond. *English Journal* 91.2 (2001): 116–17.

Fader, Ellen. Rev. of *Kit's Wilderness*, by David Almond. *School Library Journal* 46.3 (2000): 233.

Fisher, Enicia. Rev. of *Kit's Wilderness*, by David Almond. *Christian Science Monitor* 92.94 (2000): 15.

Odean, Kathleen. Rev. of *Kit's Wilderness*, by David Almond. *Book* May 2001: 80.

Rev. of *Kit's Wilderness*, by David Almond. *Cooperative Children's Book Center Choice* 2001. *Children's Literature Reviews, Children's Literature Comprehensive Database*. Online. 29 May 2003.

Wagner, Erica. "Could a Children's Book Win the Booker?" Rev. of *Kit's Wilderness*, by David Almond. *The Times* [London] 20 May 1999. *Lexis-Nexis*. Online. 4 June 2003.

Secret Heart

Arkoff, Vicki. Rev. of *Secret Heart*, by David Almond. *Midwest Book Review* March 2003. *Children's Literature Reviews, Children's Literature Comprehensive Database*. Online. 11 March 2005.

Bearden, Elaine. Rev. of *Secret Heart*, by David Almond. *Bulletin of the Center for Children's Books* 56.4 (2002). *Children's Literature Reviews, Children's Literature Comprehensive Database*. Online. 11 March 2005.

Cart, Michael. Rev. of *Secret Heart*, by David Almond. *Booklist* 99.3 (2002). *Children's Literature Reviews, Children's Literature Comprehensive Database*. Online. 11 March 2005.

Rev. of *Secret Heart*, by David Almond. *Horn Book Guide* 14.1 (2003). *Children's Literature Reviews, Children's Literature Comprehensive Database*. Online. 11 March 2005.

Rev. of *Secret Heart*, by David Almond. *Kirkus Reviews* 70.17 (2002). *Children's Literature Reviews, Children's Literature Comprehensive Database*. Online. 11 March 2005.

Rohrlick, Paula. Rev. of *Secret Heart*, by David Almond. *KLIATT Review* 36.6 (2002). *Children's Literature Reviews, Children's Literature Comprehensive Database*. Online. 11 March 2005.

Spring, Kit. Rev. of *Secret Heart*, by David Almond. *The Observer* [London] 11 March 2001. *Guardian Unlimited*. Online. 26 August 2005, http://observer.guardian.co.uk/review/story/0,6903,449778,00.html.

Williams, Sherrie. Rev. of *Secret Heart*, by David Almond. *VOYA* 25.5 (2002). *Children's Literature Reviews, Children's Literature Comprehensive Database*. Online. 11 March 2005.

Secret Heart: The Play (Adapted for the Stage by Amanda Dalton)

Cavendish, Dominic. "Tiger without Teeth Stalks a Shattered Dreamscape." Rev. of *Secret Heart: The Play*, adap. Amanda Dalton. *The Daily Telegraph* [London] 12 December 2002. *NewsBank*. Online. 1 September 2005.

Kingston, Jeremy. Rev. of *Secret Heart: The Play*, adap. Amanda Dalton. *The Times* [London] 12 December 2002. *NewsBank*. Online. 1 September 2005.

Skellig

Bush, Elizabeth. Rev. of *Skellig*, by David Almond. *Bulletin of the Center for Children's Books* 52.7 (1999). *Children's Literature Reviews, Children's Literature Comprehensive Database*. Online. 29 May 2003.

Cooper, Ilene. Rev. of *Skellig*, by David Almond. *Booklist* 95.11 (1999). *Children's Literature Reviews, Children's Literature Comprehensive Database*. Online. 29 May 2003.

Klass, Perri. Rev. of *Skellig*, by David Almond. *New York Times* 6 June 1999, sec. 7: 49.

Rev. of *Skellig*, by David Almond. *Kirkus Reviews* 15 December 1998. *Lexis-Nexis*. Online. 17 May 2005.

Rosser, Claire. Rev. of *Skellig*, by David Almond. *KLIATT Review* 33.1 (1999). *Children's Literature Reviews, Children's Literature Comprehensive Database*. Online. 29 May 2003.

Skellig: The Play

Billington, Michael. "Trevor Nunn's Tetchy Tramp: *Skellig*." Rev. of *Skellig: The Play*, by David Almond. *The Guardian* [London] 5 December 2003. *NewsBank*. Online. 1 September 2005.

Gross, John. Rev. of *Skellig: The Play*, by David Almond. *The Sunday Telegraph* [London] 14 December 2003. *NewsBank*. Online. 1 September 2005.

Nightingale, Benedict. Rev. of *Skellig: The Play*, by David Almond. *The Times* [London] 5 December 2003. *NewsBank*. Online. 1 September 2005.

Spencer, Charles. "To the Heart of a Children's Classic." Rev. of *Skellig: The Play*, by David Almond. *The Daily Telegraph* [London] 5 December 2003. *Lexis-Nexis*. Online. 1 September 2005.

Selected Websites

Hodder Children's Books. *David Almond*. 11 May 2005, www.davidalmond.com/.

Random House. *David Almond*. 11 May 2005, www.randomhouse.com/features/davidalmond/.

Other Works Cited

"Allotment." Def. 4. *The Oxford English Dictionary*. 2nd ed. New York: Oxford University Press, 1989.

Arbel, Ilil. "Rabbi Loeb." *Encyclopedia Mythica*. Online. 2 August 2005, www.pantheon.org/mythica.html.

Auerbach, Nina. *Private Theatricals: The Lives of the Victorians*. Cambridge, MA: Harvard University Press, 1990.

Bakhtin, M. M. *The Dialogic Imagination: Four Essays*. Ed. Michael Holquist. Trans. Caryl Emerson and Michael Holquist. Austin, TX: University of Texas Press, 1981.

Bettelheim, Bruno. *The Uses of Enchantment: The Meaning and Importance of Fairy Tales*. New York: Knopf, 1976; New York: Vintage–Random, 1989.

Blake, William. *The Complete Poetry and Prose of William Blake*. Ed. David V. Erdman. Newly rev. ed. New York: Anchor Books, 1988.

Bowers, Maggie Ann. *Magic(al) Realism*. New York: Routledge, 2004.

Coles, Robert. *The Call of Stories: Teaching and the Moral Imagination*. Boston: Houghton Mifflin, 1989.

Fallon, J. E. "Mary Magdalene, St." *New Catholic Encyclopedia*. 2nd ed. Detroit: Gale, 2003.

Faris, Wendy B. *Ordinary Enchantments: Magical Realism and the Remystification of Narrative*. Nashville, TN: Vanderbilt University Press, 2004.

García Márquez, Gabriel. "A Very Old Man with Enormous Wings: A Tale for Children." *Collected Stories*. By Gabriel García Márquez. Trans. Gregory Rabassa and J. S. Bernstein. New York: Perennial Classics, 1999. 217–25.

"Liminal." *The American Heritage Dictionary of the English Language*. 4th ed. Boston: Houghton Mifflin, 2000.

Lindemans, Micha F. "Golem." *Encyclopedia Mythica*. 2 August 2005, www.pantheon.org/mythica.html.

Pelikan, Jaroslav Jan. "Mary." *Encyclopedia Britannica Online*. 4 August 2005.

Rorty, Richard. *Contingency, Irony, and Solidarity*. New York: Cambridge University Press, 1989.

Sedgwick, Eve Kosofsky. *Between Men: English Literature and Male Homosocial Desire*. New York: Columbia University Press, 1985.

Trites, Roberta Seelinger. *Disturbing the Universe: Power and Repression in Adolescent Literature*. Iowa City, IA: University of Iowa Press, 2000.

Zamora, Lois Parkinson, and Wendy B. Faris, eds. *Magical Realism: Theory, History, Community*. Durham, NC: Duke University Press, 1995.

~

Index

"1962," 5

acting, 7, 46, 51, 57, 58, 59, 61, 129, 130
allegory, 66, 83, 87
Almond, David: attitude toward school, 1–2, 39, 49n7, 105–6; childhood, 1–3; family, 3, 7, 15–32 (passim); marriage, 3; relationship with grandfather, 3, 79, 101; religious beliefs, 120, 121, 129; teaching career, 3–4, 39; writing career, 1, 3. *See also Counting Stars*
Almond, Freya Grace (daughter), ix, 4
Ammon, Bette, 52
"The Angel of Chilside Road," 22–23, 31
angels, 17, 22–23, 27–28, 33–48 (passim), 74, 100; guardian, 29, 75; vision of, 120–21, 124
Anglican Church, 21
animation, 76, 116–17, 119, 121, 126
anti-war novel, 97, 99
apocalypse, 98, 107–8
Arkoff, Vicki, 82
art, 7, 52, 56–62, 115, 125–27
arthritis: doctor, 42–43; of mother (Catherine), 22, 23, 24, 25; of Skellig, 35
artist, 116, 125–27
Auerbach, Nina, 54
authority, 105–6, 110

"The Baby," 28–29, 31, 101
Bakhtin, Mikhail, 32n11, 80
Bamford, Janet, 81
"Barbara's Photographs," 23
Bearden, Elaine, 82
"Beating the Bounds," 15, 17, 19, 21–22
"Behind the Billboards," 26

Blake, William, 37–41, 47, 81, 86–87; "The Angel," 40–41; "English Encouragement of Art," 38; "Infant Joy," 41; "Night," 39–40; "The School-Boy," 38–39; *Songs of Innocence and of Experience*, 38, 41, 86; "The Tyger," 38, 86
Bloom, Harold, 53
Bloom, Susan P., 52
books, 85
Borges, Jorge Luis, 5
Boston Globe–Horn Book Award for Fiction and Poetry, 97, 99, 108
Bowers, Maggie Ann, 10, 130
Brennan, Geraldine, 7, 57, 61, 62, 72
"Buffalo Camel Llama Zebra Ass," 24, 79
bullies, 26, 103, 110, 116
Burma, 5, 97, 101, 107, 108, 109
Bush, Elizabeth, 16, 34, 52

Card, Timnah, 99
Carnegie Medal, 34
carnival, 24, 90
carnivalesque, 80
Carpentier, Alejo, 8
Cart, Michael, 82
Catholic Church, 2, 17, 20–31 (passim), 97, 105–8 (passim), 121–25. *See also* Almond, David, religious beliefs
Cavendish, Dominic, 94n6
"Chickens," 26–27
The Christian Science Monitor, 52
Christianity, 83, 90
Chronicles of Narnia, 88
circus, 81–92 (passim)
clairvoyance, 81
Clay, x, 115–27, 130
clay, 72, 115–27 (passim)
"A Clean Well-Lighted Place," 2
cloning, 117
Coghlan, Susanna, 98
Cold War, 101, 103
community, 7, 28–31, 57–62 (passim), 101, 106, 123
confession, 122–23, 127
Cooper, Ilene, 34, 52, 66, 98
Cooperative Children's Book Center Choices, 52
Counting Stars, x, 3, 5, 6, 10, 15–31, 67, 79, 101, 105, 115, 121, 130, 131
"Counting the Stars," 19–21, 30
Craig, Amanda, 99
creativity: as theme, 7, 8, 129; in *Clay*, 115, 125–27; in *Heaven Eyes*, 66, 70, 72, 77; in *Kit's Wilderness*, 51–62 (passim)
Cuban Missile Crisis, 5, 97, 98, 99, 107, 109–10, 118
cultural appropriation, 109

Dalton, Amanda, 94n6
Dalton, Michael, 81
damaged people, 65, 67, 68, 70–74, 85
death: as theme, 3, 5, 7, 9; in *Counting Stars*, 15, 22, 28; in *The Fire-Eaters*, 109; in *Heaven Eyes*, 66, 69, 74–77; in *Kit's Wilderness*, 51, 55, 56–57, 62; of Barbara Almond (sister), 2, 7, 17, 19, 22–23, 25, 27; of father James Almond (father), 2, 3, 7, 17, 20–21, 24, 25, 79
Del Negro, Janice M., 69
demons, 30, 87, 100, 124, 130

devils, 58, 120
discernment of magic, 37, 38, 40–41, 42, 44–45, 81, 86, 87, 88–93 (passim), 129
Donelson, Ken, 52
dreams: in *Clay*, 119; in *Counting Stars*, 17, 23, 27–28, 31; in *The Fire-Eaters*, 102, 104; in *Heaven Eyes*, 75; in *Kate, the Cat and the Moon*, 93; in *Kit's Wilderness*, 55, 56, 61; in *Secret Heart*, 81–89 (passim); in *Skellig*, 33, 38, 40, 41–46; of authorship, 131–32; waking, 43–45

Eccleshare, Julie, 93
Enlightenment, 80

Fader, Ellen, 52
family: as theme, 5, 7; in *Counting Stars*, 15, 16–22, 25–26, 31; in *The Fire-Eaters*, 101, 108; in *Heaven Eyes*, 71, 75; in *Kit's Wilderness*, 57, 60, 62; in *Secret Heart*, 81–82, 90. *See also* Almond, David, family
fantasy, 66
Faris, Wendy B., 9, 11, 81
Felling, 18, 21, 28, 115, 122, 123, 125, 131
fiction, 17, 31
"Fiesta," 6, 101
The Fire-Eaters (film), 131
The Fire-Eaters (novel), x, 1, 5, 10, 97–112, 115, 118, 121, 125, 130
fire-eating, 6, 87, 97–112 (passim)
Frankenstein, 117–18, 127
Freud, Sigmund, 53, 120
"The Fuselier," 25

Gardner, Lyn, 66
gender, 104
Geordie dialect, 99
ghosts, 5, 25, 52, 55, 56, 59, 68, 76
God, 20–21, 102, 106, 117, 120–21, 125, 126, 129
god, 120
Goldsworthy, Sally, 79
Golem, 116–17, 127
grief, 79–81
grotesque, 98, 99
Guardian Award for Children's Fiction, 99
Guy Fawkes Night, 111, 113n18

Hawthorne, Nathaniel, 126
Heaven Eyes (film), 131, 132n10
Heaven Eyes (novel), x, 1, 9, 15, 65–77, 81, 83, 84, 86, 112, 115, 116, 119, 125, 130
Hemingway, Ernest, 2
heteroglossia, 32n11, 80
history, 62, 70, 88. *See also* past
The Horn Book, 82, 99
The Horn Book Guide, 66
Huckleberry Finn, 69
hypnotism, 116, 118–19, 124, 126

Id, 120
identity: as role playing, 58, 74; as theme, 6, 7, 9, 129; fluidity of, 53, 54, 72–73, 87, 90–91; in *The Fire-Eaters*, 103–5; in *Heaven Eyes*, 65, 67, 68, 70–77; in *Kit's Wilderness*, 51, 55, 56, 61, 62; in *Secret Heart*, 81–92 (passim)
illustration, 7, 38, 42, 51, 58–59, 61, 62, 125, 129, 131
images, 108–12

imagination: as theme: 7–8, 9, 11, 130; in *Clay*, 115; in *Counting Stars*, 19, 22–24, 27, 28; in *The Fire-Eaters*, 99; in *Kate, the Cat and the Moon*, 93; in *Kit's Wilderness*, 55, 59–60; in *Secret Heart*, 85; in *Skellig*, 42, 48; in *Wild Girl, Wild Boy*, 80
individual, 28–31
inner child, 61
intertextuality, 33, 116, 131

"Jack Law," 30–31, 101
Jesus Christ, 102, 124
Johnston, Rosemary Ross, 80
"Jonadab," 17, 25–26
Jones, Nicolette, 93, 99
journeys, 17, 25–27, 68–70, 74, 76, 83, 93

Kate, the Cat and the Moon, x, 92–93, 131
Keely Bay, 98, 99, 103, 109, 111
Kennedy, John F., 107, 109
A *Kind of Heaven* (short story collection), ix, 4, 5, 101
"A Kind of Heaven" (short story), 5
Kingston, Jeremy, 94n6
Kirkus Reviews, 16, 34, 66, 82, 99
Kit's Wilderness, x, 1, 3, 7, 9, 15, 51–62, 65, 67, 69, 70, 84, 99, 107, 115, 119, 125, 130
Klass, Perri, 34
Kruschev, Nikita, 107, 109

Lambert, Stephen, 93
Lesesne, Teri S., 99
Lewis, C. S., 88
library, 2, 27, 131
liminal territory, 11, 12, 55, 70, 84
"Loosa Fine," 29–30, 31, 101
"Lucy Blue," 5
Lyric Theatre, Hammersmith, London, x, 46, 79, 81

magic: as theme, 6–12, 129–32; dark side of, 115, 116, 118–21; in *Clay*, 115, 116, 118–21; in *Counting Stars*, 17, 19, 28; in *The Fire-Eaters*, 99, 101, 102; in *Heaven Eyes*, 67–70 (passim), 74–77 (passim); in *Kate, the Cat and the Moon*, 93; in *Kit's Wilderness*, 58, 60; in *Secret Heart*, 81–92 (passim); in *Skellig*, 34–48 (passim), 44–47 (passim). *See also* discernment of magic; mysticism
magic realism, 8, 45. *See also* magical realism, Marvelous Real
magical realism: as mode, 6–7, 8–12, 129–32; in *Clay*, 115; in *Heaven Eyes*, 65, 66, 76; in *Kate, the Cat and the Moon*, 93; in *Kit's Wilderness*, 52; in *Secret Heart*, 84, 89; in *Skellig*, 33, 35–37. *See also* magic realism, Marvelous Real
Maguire, Gregory, 16
Makover, Todd, 131
male homosocial desire, 62
Mark, Jan, 99
Márquez, Gabriel García, 5, 8–9, 35–37
"Marvelous Real," 8. *See also* magic realism; magical realism
McLoughlin, William, 16
Melville, Herman, 69
memory: as theme, 7, 9, 130, 132; in *Counting Stars*, 15, 17, 19, 22–24,

27, 28, 31; in *Heaven Eyes*, 65, 67, 68, 71, 73, 75, 76, 77; in *Kit's Wilderness*, 56. *See also* photographs
Michael L. Printz: Award, 1, 8, 53, 55, 60, 129; Honor Book, 1, 34
"The Middle of the World," 17–19
Moby Dick, 69
monster, 115–27 (passim)
Munat, Florence H., 66, 69
"My Mother's Photographs," 23–24
mysticism: in *Clay*, 124, 125; in *Counting Stars*, 15, 29, 30; in *The Fire-Eaters*, 90, 100, 105; in *Heaven Eyes*, 66, 75, 76; in *Secret Heart*, 81, 84, 87, 89; in *Skellig*, 40, 41. *See also* spirituality
myth, 68–70, 88, 116–17

names, 54, 55, 72–74
narrative, power of, 112, 129. *See also* stories
narrator: female, 68; third-person, 82
nature, 24, 40, 79–81, 85, 89, 91, 102
Nelson, Debra, 98
Nestle Smarties Book Prize, 99. *See also* Smarties Book Prize
Newcastle, 1, 3, 4, 81, 99, 101, 111
Nietzsche, Friedrich, 53
Norwich, 3
novels, 46
Nunn, Trevor, 46, 47

Odean, Kathleen, 52
Oedipal conflict, 87
orphans, 65–77, 119
outcasts, 17, 18, 28–31, 81, 85, 102, 118

Palmer, Sarah Jane (wife), 4
pantheism, 81
Panurge, ix, 4
past, 67, 69, 70, 73, 74–77. *See also* history
photographs: in *Clay*, 125; in *Counting Stars*, 23–24, 28–29; in *The Fire-Eaters*, 98, 104, 106, 108–12; in *Heaven Eyes*, 71, 74–75; in *Secret Heart*, 89. *See also* memory
physical realm, 17, 19, 27–28, 30, 31, 40, 41
place, 7, 15, 17–22, 52, 108
polyphony, 17, 32n11
post-traumatic stress syndrome, 101
primitivism, 89, 102, 105
prophet, 88
Protestant, 116, 117, 120
Pullman, Philip, 16

"Rabbi Loeb and the Golem of Prague," 117, 127
Rampa, T. Lobsong, 27
rationality, 80
realism, 66, 81, 99, 100, 130, 131
rebirth, 70, 74–77
reincarnation, 81, 87, 90
religion, 24, 118, 120–21, 124. *See also* Almond, David, religious beliefs; Anglican Church; Catholic Church
religious: conflict, 117, 120; persecution, 117
resistance, 110–11
resurrection, 76, 102
ritual, 89–90
Rochman, Hazel, 16

Roh, Franz, 8
Rohrlick, Paula, 82
Romantic child, 76
Rorty, Richard, 53, 62
Rosser, Claire, 34
Royal Exchange Theatre, Manchester, x, 94n6

school: in *Clay*, 119, 120–21, 125; in *Counting Stars*, 30–31; in *The Fire-Eaters*, 97–98, 102–6, 108, 110–11; in *Secret Heart*, 81, 86; in *Skellig*, 38–39, 47; in *Wild Girl, Wild Boy*, 80. *See also* Almond, David, attitude toward school
science, 117–18
Secret Heart (novel), x, 7, 8, 9–10, 46, 80, 81–92, 101, 111, 125, 130
Secret Heart (play), x, 94n6
Sedgwick, Eve Kosofsky, 62
Sendak, Maurice, 93
sexuality, 26–28, 100
shape-shifting, 81, 86–87, 90, 92
Shelley, Mary, 117–18
Skellig (film), 131
Skellig (novel), ix, x, 1, 4, 6, 7, 8–9, 11, 15, 20, 27, 29, 33–48, 52, 65, 70, 79, 80, 100, 130, 131
Skellig (opera), 131
Skellig (play), 46–48
Sleepless Nights, ix, 4–5
Smarties Book Prize, 1, 15. *See also* Nestle Smarties Book Prize
social: class, 103–6, 108, 110; issues, 117–18
society, 28–31, 69, 71, 86; criticism of, 65, 71, 77, 100, 105–6, 130
spirituality: in *Clay*, 124, 125, in *Counting Stars*, 17, 19, 27–28, 31, in *The Fire-Eaters*, 100, in *Heaven Eyes*, 67, 68, 69, 76, in *Secret Heart*, 88, 90, in *Skellig*, 40, of Almond's adolescent characters, 129. *See also* mysticism
"Spotlight," 5
St. Sebastian, 102
stories: as theme, 7, 129–30; in *Clay*, 121, 127; in *Counting Stars*, 15, 17, 19; in *The Fire-Eaters*, 111–12; in *Heaven Eyes*, 65, 67, 70, 71, 74–75, 77; in *Kit's Wilderness*, 55, 57, 59–62; in *Secret Heart*, 85, 88, 92; in *Skellig*, 46
Stories from the Middle of the World, 4
storytelling, 47–48, 59–62, 77, 125, 131
"The Subtle Body," 27
symbolism, 82

theater, 46, 48, 130
Threlfall, David, 46
"The Time Machine," 24
totemism, 81
transformation, 83, 84, 86–87, 91–92, 93, 116–18, 127, 130. *See also* shape-shifting
Trites, Roberta Seelinger, 56, 108, 109
truth, 17, 31, 33
Twain, Mark, 69
Tyne River, 65; as symbol, 69, 76

University of East Anglia, 3

"A Very Old Man with Enormous Wings," 8–9, 35–37
Virgin Mary, 29, 123

Wagner, Erica, 16, 52
war: games, 107, 118; with Iraq, 97, 108, 118, 130; World War II, 97, 100, 101, 107, 108
wasteland, 84
Where the Wild Things Are, 93
Where Your Wings Were (short story collection), x, 6, 15
"Where Your Wings Were" (short story), 5, 17, 27–28
Whitbread Children's Book of the Year Award, 1, 34, 99
Wild Girl, Wild Boy, x, 3, 46, 55, 70, 79–81, 85, 91, 125, 131
wilderness, 51, 54–62 (passim), 70, 81, 87, 93
wildness, 84–85
Williams, Sherrie, 16, 82
Wilson, Wils, 94n6
writing, 17, 29, 51, 59, 61, 62, 73, 80, 129

Young Vic Theatre, London, x, 46

Zamora, Lois Parkinson, 11

~

About the Author

Don Latham is an assistant professor in the College of Information at Florida State University, where he teaches courses in young adult literature and information services. He has published articles on Peter Sís, Lois Lowry, and John Donovan in *Children's Literature in Education*, *Children's Literature*, *The Lion and the Unicorn*, and *The ALAN Review*. His research focuses on the role of magical realism in young adult literature and the role of literature in shaping young adults' identities. He is active in the Young Adult Library Services Association and the Association for Library Service to Children and has served as president of the Friends of the Florida State University Libraries. He lives in Tallahassee, Florida.